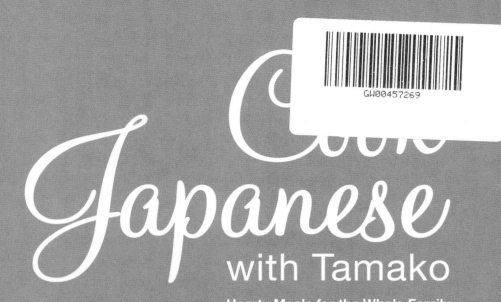

Japanese
with Tamako

Hearty Meals for the Whole Family

**TAMAKO
SAKAMOTO**

photography by Noriko Yamaguchi

mc Marshall Cavendish
Cuisine

All photographs by Noriko Yamaguchi except for those on pages 22, 24, 26, 84, 96, 100, 102
and 114 from the Sakamoto family album.

Published by Marshall Cavendish Cuisine
An imprint of Marshall Cavendish International

Other Marshall Cavendish Offices:

Marshall Cavendish Corporation. 99 White Plains Road, Tarrytown NY 10591-9001, USA • Marshall
Cavendish International (Thailand) Co Ltd. 253 Asoke, 12th Flr, Sukhumvit 21 Road, Klongtoey Nua,
Wattana, Bangkok 10110, Thailand • Marshall Cavendish (Malaysia) Sdn Bhd, Times Subang, Lot 46,
Subang Hi-Tech Industrial Park, Batu Tiga, 40000 Shah Alam, Selangor Darul Ehsan, Malaysia

Marshall Cavendish is a trademark of Times Publishing Limited

National Library Board, Singapore Cataloguing-in-Publication Data
Sakamoto, Tamako.
Cook Japanese with Tamako : hearty meals for the whole family / Tamako Sakamoto.
– Singapore : Marshall Cavendish Cuisine, 2013.
pages cm
ISBN : 978-981-4516-11-2 (paperback)

1. Cooking, Japanese. 2. Sakamoto, Tamako – Family.
3. Women journalists – Family relationships – Japan.
4. Families – Japan. I. Title.

TX724.5.J3
641.5952 -- dc23   OCN857708916

Printed in Singapore by Craft Print International Ltd

"I planted, Apollos watered, but God caused the growth."

I Corinthians 3:6

Contents

Introduction

What comes to mind when you think of Japanese food? Neatly placed jewel-like sushi, thin, almost transparent slices of beef for shabu-shabu or crispy, deep-fried tempura, beautifully arranged on a plate?

While it is true that the Japanese have long enjoyed such traditional food, you will discover, in this book, that Japanese mothers like myself have a much larger repertory of home-style dishes made with fresh, seasonal ingredients. We also enjoy foods from other countries, using native Japanese produce as necessary. On any family dining table, you are also bound to find dishes with roots from other countries along with traditional Japanese dishes.

This book contains the articles and recipes that have appeared in my column, *Taste of Home*, which started in 2006, in *The Daily Yomiuri* (now named *The Japan News*), an English newspaper published by *The Yomiuri Shimbun*. The four chapters in the book are arranged chronologically, featuring recipes from the first four years of the column. Since my four children often feature in the articles, you will be able to trace their growth through the chapters.

I am not a professional chef, but I am a mother in a family of six. Most of the recipes in this book are ones I learnt from my mother and grandmothers or ideas I got from my friends. Some are my original recipes and some are well known traditional dishes that Japanese mothers often prepare. In essence, these recipes can be likened to comfortable cotton T-shirts rather than kimonos made of silk.

After I left my full-time job to stay home and take care of my growing family, I constantly felt that these incredibly busy days caring for my young children would last forever. The laundry piled up, the bags of groceries were quickly consumed, and the meals I spent hours preparing disappeared within minutes. But it was while I was raising my children that the recipes in this book and the stories that go with them were born.

I don't keep a diary or maintain a blog to keep a record of what goes on in my life, so it was not until I reread my old manuscripts to publish this book that I realized the days I felt would never end were actually changing all the time. A family is in constant transformation. As my children grow up and leave home, the amount of food I prepare will gradually be reduced. The days of struggling to prepare incredible amounts of food will not last for the rest of my life. So, I'll enjoy these days of cooking for great appetites and be thankful for the joy that we are able to share around the table.

I am delighted that you have found this book and I hope you will enjoy preparing these dishes with a Japanese taste of home.

Tamako Sakamoto

A Growing Family

A cabbage dish fit for surprise guests

I cook for six as the minimum number every day. The headcount includes my husband, three boys and a girl. The children, aged six through 13, are always hungry. In the morning, I pack lunch in a bento box for one of my sons and prepare breakfast for my other family members who leave home one after another.

The children head straight to the kitchen when they come home. As they are all involved in sports activities, they spend most of their time training or expecting some food at home. Even my youngest son, who just started elementary school this spring says he wants to eat some 'real' food instead of sweet snacks before dinner.

I also make a dinner box twice a week, which my 10-year-old daughter takes to her cram school. For my husband who comes home late at night without having eaten anything since lunch, I try to prepare balanced dishes. My parents also join us from time to time.

Thanks to these daily tasks, it does not matter to me if my children bring friends home and there are additional kids at our dinner table, or if friends drop by unannounced, since I usually prepare a lot of food to make sure that everybody gets enough. We enjoy sitting around the big family table and my children seem happy to share their dinner with visitors, although they usually fight to make sure they get a large portion for themselves!

Here is a good recipe to try especially when you have unexpected visitors dropping by. It is a simmered dish of cabbage leaves layered with minced meat, which I learnt from a chef I know. It is easy to cook compared to rolled cabbage which uses similar ingredients. With this dish, you do not have to worry about the exact number of guests as you can serve the dish by cutting it into wedges as you would a cake.

Although it is a Western-style dish, I make it a rule to add a tablespoon of soy sauce to the stock to give it a touch of extra flavour. This dish goes well served either with bread or rice.

I usually use 900 g (2 lb) of minced meat and $1^1/_2$ heads of cabbage to cook enough for a hungry crowd. Any leftovers can be cut up and stored in the freezer with a little of the soup—although in my experience, there are usually hardly any leftovers!

Simmered Layered Cabbage   Serves 6–8

1¹/₂ medium cabbages

60 g (2 oz) panko breadcrumbs

120 ml (¹/₂ cup) milk

1 onion

900 g (2 lb) minced pork and beef mixture

1 egg

1¹/₂ tsp salt

ground black pepper

3 bouillon cubes

1 Tbsp Japanese soy sauce

600 ml (2¹/₂ cups) hot water

2–3 bay leaves

5 slices bacon, roughly chopped

herbes de Provence or other herbs, optional

1. Carve out the hard core of each cabbage and discard. Peel the cabbage leaves carefully and parboil for 2–3 minutes or until pliable. Drain, then slice off the hard veins. Soak the panko in the milk. Peel and mince the onion. In a bowl, mix the minced meat with the onion, panko and egg. Season with salt and pepper and mix well.

2. Spread one third of the cabbage leaves flat in a flat-bottom pot. I usually use an oval pot measuring 27 x 22 cm (10 x 8¹/₂ inches). Place half the meat mixture on top of the cabbage leaves and spread out evenly. Smooth the surface. Repeat the process to make cabbage and meat layers, ending with a layer of cabbage. Press down with your hands to compact the layers and smooth the surface.

3. Add the bouillon cubes and soy sauce to the 600 ml (2¹/₂ cups) hot water. Pour the liquid over the layers of cabbage. Place the bay leaves and bacon on top. You may add a sprinkling of herbs, such as herbes de Provence for a tasty touch. Simmer covered on the stovetop for 50–60 minutes. Slice and serve.

Crisp mizuna, perfect for salad

The other day, my eight-year-old son brought home a handful of baby mizuna leaves. The children at his school are cultivating many kinds of vegetables and my son chose mizuna, taking care of his baby leaves every day. He was so proud of his first harvest and wanted everybody to have a taste, although it was obviously not enough for all of us. However, as he was so excited, I promised to cook the leaves for dinner.

Have you ever tasted fresh mizuna leaves? Mizuna used to be cultivated only in the Kyoto/Osaka region and was known as *kyona* (Kyoto green) instead of mizuna (water green). The bright green colour of the delicate leaves and the crisp but juicy texture of the white stalks fascinated the people in the Tokyo region, so now it can be found easily at any supermarket outside Kyoto/Osaka. Personally, I cannot imagine cooking without mizuna any more.

As it was originally a winter vegetable, mizuna is good simmered with *abura-age* (deep-fried tofu) or with *nabe* hot pots in the wintertime. Mizuna is available almost year round. For the spring season, I recommend this cool mizuna and tofu salad. I learnt the recipe from a younger friend at church. She whipped up the salad in just a few minutes and everybody was very impressed. It is a healthy, tasty and quick dish prepared with *chirimenjako* (small dried sardines). Crisp, lightly salted *chirimenjako* go very well with the moist and creamy tofu salad.

In the Tokyo region, little dried sardines are commonly known as *shirasuboshi*. In the Kyoto/Osaka region, they are called *chirimenjako*. *Chirimenjako* are drier and have a tougher texture than *shirasuboshi*, which are rather moist. For this recipe, be sure to use *chirimenjako*.

Although the original recipe contained no dressing, I find it goes well with sesame dressing. Feel free to experiment with your own favourite dressings. The mizuna leaves that my son brought home were very tasty and he was happy to hear the compliments from everybody at the dinner table. As I've heard that mizuna is one of the easiest vegetables to cultivate, I'm now planning to cultivate some in our garden.

DRAINING TOFU If you have enough time, I recommend wrapping the tofu in a paper towel and putting it in a sieve to drain before using.

SUBSTITUTE FOR MIZUNA Mizuna is becoming more widely available in the West, where it is sometimes known as spider mustard. If you can't get hold of it, try young mustard greens or arugula (rocket) instead.

SUBSTITUTE FOR CHIRIMENJAKO *Chirimenjako* may be found in the frozen section of Asian grocery stores. If you can't get hold of *chirimenjako*, walnuts that have been coarsely chopped and lightly sautéed are a good substitute in terms of texture.

Mizuna and Tofu Salad   Serves 6–8

300 g (10¹/₂ oz) soft tofu, drained
   (see Note)

200 g (7 oz) *mizuna*, cut into 4-cm
   (1¹/₂-inch) lengths

salt, to taste

2 Tbsp sesame oil

30 g (1 oz) *chirimenjako*

sesame dressing or dressing
   of your choice

1. Using your hands, crumble the tofu and gently combine
   with the *mizuna* in a mixing bowl. Lightly season with salt.
   Arrange the *mizuna* and tofu mixture in a serving bowl.

2. In a frying pan, heat the oil over medium heat and add the
   chirimenjako. Carefully cook the *chirimenjako* until crisp
   but before they colour. Put the fried *chirimenjako* on top
   of the *mizuna* and tofu and lightly mix.

3. Serve while the *chirimenjako* are still sizzling and crisp.
   Enjoy with or without dressing.

15

Trapped in the lure of asari clams

I think it was the Sunday before the Golden Week holidays when my husband suggested that we go *shiohigari* (clam gathering) at a nearby beach as the weather was perfect for it. It was unusual for him to suggest that kind of outdoor activity and I agreed immediately as I knew the children would enjoy the activity. However, as the thought sank in, I began to worry that everyone in the area would probably have come up with the same idea. The sky was clear and it was neither too hot nor too cold, meaning that the beach would be very crowded. We decided to stay home.

The next morning, a photograph on the front page of the daily newspaper jumped out at me. It was an aerial photograph taken from a helicopter, showing a beach crammed with 12,000 people doing *shiohigari*. There was a long line of people waiting to have their clams weighed before leaving the beach. (There is often a charge for the clams gathered based on weight.) It was exactly the place we had thought of going. Somehow, it seems that the Japanese are genetically programmed to want to go to the beach and collect shellfish on a fine day. Even though they can predict how horribly crowded the beaches will be,

they seem unable to resist the temptation. *Shiohigari* is indeed that much fun!

Here is my favourite recipe for preparing *asari* clams, which I learnt from a friend of my parents, Mrs Yamaguchi. I first tried this soup when she served it after a barbecue party. I was intrigued to see that she didn't cut the vegetables with a knife. Instead, she sliced most of them with a large peeler. It was impressive to watch her slice daikon radish into very thin, round pieces— something rarely seen in a Japanese kitchen. I am not sure if it was because her father was from Vietnam, but the soup tasted exotic even though it did not contain any special herbs. I usually prepare this soup with a spoonful of Thai fish sauce (*nam pla*) to give it a different flavour.

Asari clams are rich in taurine, an amino acid believed to have a good effect on the liver and I am sure the combination of *asari* clams and celery is good for anyone who may be suffering from a hangover.

SUBSTITUTE FOR ASARI CLAMS *Asari* clams are a Japanese variety of the littleneck clam. In this recipe, you can substitute *asari* clams with littleneck clams or cockles.

Asari and Celery Soup with a Twist   Serves 6–8

400 g (14 oz) *asari* clams

1 carrot

10-cm (4-inch) length daikon radish

1 stalk celery with leaves

1 leek

1 knob fresh ginger

1 clove garlic

2 tsp instant dashi powder

2 litres (8 cups) water

1 Tbsp Japanese soy sauce

1 tsp Thai fish sauce (*nam pla*)

1 Tbsp sake

1 tsp salt

ground white pepper

1. Wash and scrub the clams. To remove sand from freshly gathered clams, cover them well with salted water (1 tsp salt per 240 ml / 1 cup of water) and leave to soak for 2–3 hours in the refrigerator before using.

2. Peel and cut the carrot and daikon into thin, fan-shaped pieces or thinly slice them with a peeler. Trim, peel and cut the celery stalk into 5-cm (2-inch) wide pieces and set aside. Cut the celery leaves into 1-cm ($^{1}/_{2}$-inch) wide strips. Thinly slice the leek on the diagonal. Peel and slice the ginger. Peel and slice the garlic.

3. Put the carrot, daikon, chopped celery stalk, ginger, garlic and dashi powder in a pot with the 2 litres (8 cups) of water. Cook over medium heat for about 20 minutes or until the vegetables are tender. Add the clams, celery leaves, leek, soy sauce, fish sauce, sake, salt and pepper. Skim off any foam from the surface and cook for 2–3 minutes or until all the clams are open. Dish out and serve.

Dressing up plain tuna as tasty toro

The other day, my husband had a day off work and we went to a sushi restaurant for lunch. As the children were at school, we had a quiet lunch together. Frankly, you need to be prepared to spend a lot if you bring your growing children to a sushi restaurant, as they eat an incredible amount. The last time I took my eldest son to the restaurant, I had given him a regular meal before we left home. Still, he wolfed down a lot of sushi. When we next bring all four children to eat sushi, we will seriously consider stopping by at a fast food restaurant beforehand to lessen their appetites.

Although both my husband and I like toro (the fatty belly of tuna), we usually have to forego such expensive cuts. However, until four years ago, we were able to enjoy as much toro as we liked once a year.

Mr Yoshinaga, a close friend of my parents, used to raise tuna in Spain. The fish would be caught, brought alive to the coast and raised until they were ready for sale. This way, there would be a ready supply of tuna, in perfect condition, whenever there was demand. While he was involved in the business, Mr Yoshinaga would send us a huge box containing the best cuts of tuna once a year. Whenever the wonderful gift arrived, my mother would hold a tuna party for the whole family.

Although we had a hard time cutting the slabs of tuna into thin slices—not exactly regular work for housewives—the children loved to watch the exciting process. On that special day, even the younger ones were allowed to have their share of *chutoro* (medium fatty toro) and *otoro* (the most fatty and expensive cut of toro).

When Mr Yoshinaga passed away four years ago, we were saddened because we had so many memories of him going back to the days when I was a child. After a while, we also realized that we would never be able to hold the annual tuna party any more. However, he gave us wonderful memories of family events when we all got together to enjoy precious, tasty toro.

As my children love tuna, I get it for them once in a while. Tuna and avocado *donburi* is one of their favourite dishes. The dish is really amazing since even the lean part of tuna tastes a little like toro when mixed with avocado. I am not sure if my children still remember the taste of really good toro, but they seem happy with this quick avocado dish.

VARIATION Shredded nori makes a good topping for this dish. You can also add 3 Tbsp finely ground toasted white sesame seeds to the soy sauce mixture. The dish will then be known as *gomazuke* (tuna in sesame-flavoured dip) *donburi*.

Tuna and Avocado Donburi   Serves 4

400 g (14 oz) lean fresh tuna

4 Tbsp Japanese soy sauce

2 Tbsp sake

1 Tbsp mirin

1/4 tsp wasabi

1 large avocado

4 *donburi* bowls, about two-thirds filled with cooked Japanese rice (page 126)

2 tsp toasted white sesame seeds

daikon sprouts or shiso leaves, for garnish

4 fresh raw egg yolks

1. Cut the tuna into small cubes. Combine the soy sauce, sake, mirin and wasabi and soak the tuna in the mixture. Peel the avocado and cut into small cubes.

2. Arrange the tuna and avocado on top of the bowls of rice and pour the remaining liquid over each bowl. Sprinkle with the sesame seeds and garnish with daikon sprouts or shiso. Top with the raw egg yolks and serve.

A vegetable dish for your next barbecue

Real summer is almost upon us as the rainy season nears its end. During this season, we often have barbecues in the garden. I love barbecues because everybody chips in to help prepare the food and I do not have to wash many dishes afterward. My eldest son usually helps his father start the fire. My daughter makes *onigiri* (rice balls) and the younger boys wash and cut the vegetables. So all I need to do is arrange everything on a huge plate.

There used to be just one problem. Although I usually prepare a variety of vegetables to go with the meat and seafood, the kids would only eat their favourite food, which was typically the meat and especially the sausages. I tried to put vegetables on their plates whenever they had a second helping of meat, but nobody would eat them out of choice. As a result, the grill would always be stacked with dried-up vegetables.

I soon found a solution when I was preparing to cook foil-baked salmon with enoki mushrooms. This dish, topped with a chunk of butter, is popular among the children and I wondered what it would be like if I made similar servings of vegetables wrapped in foil.

At our next barbecue, I put some eggplant (aubergine), asparagus, mushrooms and a cherry tomato on a sheet of aluminium foil, seasoned them with salt, pepper and olive oil, and wrapped them up. I told my children to have a portion of the foil-baked vegetables before taking another serving of meat. But I hardly needed to force them. The dish turned out to be more popular than I had expected as the vegetables were so moist and tasty. Thanks to this foil-wrapped dish, my children now enjoy a balanced barbecue dinner and I no longer have to worry about leftover dried-up vegetables.

VARIATION Grilling in foil (*hoiru yaki*) is a cooking method that works well for all kinds of ingredients. Try creating your own grilled parcels and surprise your family and friends at your next barbecue. Here are some of my recommendations:

- Salmon and enoki mushrooms. Put a salmon fillet on a piece of foil and top with trimmed enoki mushrooms. Season with salt and black pepper. Sprinkle with 1 tsp sake and top with some butter before wrapping up. Serve with lemon and soy sauce or ponzu sauce.

- Any combination of your favourite vegetables. I recommend parboiling hard vegetables and sprinkling the lot with 1 tsp sake or olive oil before cooking.

- *Asari* clams. (Refer to page 17 for instructions on removing sand from clams). I like to cook the clams with cabbage and bean sprouts.

- Desserts, using sliced bananas or apples. You can top the fruit with marshmallows and flavour them with cinnamon sugar and lemon juice or maple syrup. Serve with ice cream.

Vegetables in Foil   Serves 6

6 asparagus spears

2 *eringi* mushrooms

2 eggplants (aubergines)

6 cherry tomatoes, trimmed

salt and ground black pepper

6 tsp olive oil

1. Trim the hard ends of the asparagus and cut each spear lengthwise in half. Boil for 2–3 minutes in lightly salted water until tender but still retaining a crisp bite. Drain.

2. Slice the mushrooms lengthwise. Cut the eggplants into halves lengthwise and slice thinly.

3. Cut 6 sheets of aluminium foil into rectangles measuring about 30 x 20 cm (12 x 8 inches). Put an equal portion of each vegetable in the centre of each sheet and season with some salt and pepper and a teaspoon of olive oil. Fold the foil over the vegetables to create a tight seal. Grill for 10 minutes or until vegetables are tender. Serve.

Nutritious summer veggies for hungry kids

Finally, the long summer vacation is over and my children have gone back to school. As everybody knows, a vacation for kids does not mean a vacation for mothers.

As a mother of four, summer is a busy time for me. My children get up hungry and expect a warm breakfast. By the time I finish washing the dishes, they have already started asking me what's for lunch. As soon as lunchtime is over, they start thinking about dinner. In addition, they ask for snacks in the mid morning and mid afternoon. Whenever one of them points at the clock, I get the feeling that my only purpose in life is to fill their bottomless stomachs. Despite this, we still have fun during the holidays.

Every summer, we go to our old house by the shore of Lake Yamanaka in Yamanashi Prefecture. There I often cook winter melon (*togan*)—a traditional vegetable that looks like a football-shaped watermelon.

When cooked, the flesh of the winter melon becomes semi-transparent and tastes somewhat like tender daikon radish. Although it is a summer vegetable, it keeps quite well and can be enjoyed even in wintertime, hence its name.

There are various kinds of winter melon but they typically weigh 3–4 kg (7–9 lb), so it is quite difficult to consume a whole melon in a single meal even for a big family like mine. Our local supermarket sells cut-up winter melons and I can get just half or a quarter, but in Yamanashi, the melons are often sold whole.

As such, whenever we are here, I usually cook winter melon soup with chicken in a large pot and have it over a couple of days until we get tired of eating it. The upside of preparing this winter melon soup, however, is that I know I have something tasty and filling on hand to feed my starving children.

The soup tastes great either hot or chilled and my children love to put cooked rice in the soup, creating a dish that they can enjoy for breakfast. It is also equally tasty to cook the soup with chicken stock instead of dashi stock. Whichever stock you chose to use, don't forget to add ginger as it adds a wonderful flavour.

Winter Melon Soup with Chicken   Serves 6–8

450 g (1 lb) winter melon

$^1/_2$ burdock root

1 Tbsp vinegar

1 Tbsp vegetable oil

200 g (7 oz) chopped or minced
chicken

1 knob fresh ginger, peeled and
chopped

2 litres (8 cups) water

1 Tbsp instant dashi powder

1 tsp Japanese soy sauce

1 tsp salt

2 Tbsp sake

1. Peel the winter melon and remove the seeds and the spongy part inside. Cut the flesh into cubes about 4–5 cm (1$^1/_2$–2 inches).

2. Wash and scrub the burdock root with a scrubbing brush, then shred. Leave in a bowl of water with 1 Tbsp vinegar for about 5 minutes. Drain and parboil for 2–3 minutes. Drain again.

3. Heat the vegetable oil in a frying pan. Add the chicken and ginger and cook for 2–3 minutes over medium heat. In a pot, bring the 2 litres (8 cups) water to a boil and add the dashi powder, burdock, winter melon and the chicken and ginger. Bring to a boil. Skim off any fat or foam from the surface from time to time. Turn the heat to low. Add the soy sauce, salt and sake. Simmer, covered, for 20–30 minutes until the winter melon is tender. Ladle into bowls and serve.

The perfect bento for sports day

The season for *undokai*, school sports day, is here once again. As soon as the autumn semester begins, children start practising for the sports event, which is one of the highlights of the school year.

Unlike formal athletic meets, *undokai* involves many interesting and traditional games such as *tama-ire* (shooting balls into a basket), *tsunahiki* (tug of war) and *kibasen* (mock cavalry battle). There are also dances, including one performed to Soranbushi, one of the most popular traditional songs in Japan.

Such events are enjoyed at all levels, from kindergartens to high schools, across the nation. They often take place on weekends around *Taiiku no Hi* (Health-Sports Day), a national holiday celebrated on the second Monday in October. *Taiiku no Hi* was established in commemoration of the 1964 Tokyo Olympic Games and used to be held on 10 October each year until it was moved to the second Monday in October, in 2000.

Let me share with you my special *undokai* memory. I gave birth to my second son on 11 October, a day after I had enjoyed dancing with my eldest son at his kindergarten *undokai*, which fell on the old date during that time. Since then, my family has always celebrated our second son's birthday on the day of *undokai*, as this is a time when all my family members can get together to enjoy the athletic event.

The Japanese often prepare *tonkatsu* (deep-fried breaded pork cutlet) for *undokai* bento boxes, and they do the same on the day of the school entrance exams. This is because the dish, *katsu* (derived from the English word, cutlet, and used to describe various deep-fried dishes) sounds like the Japanese word for win.

Of course, as a mother, it doesn't matter to me whether my children win or lose. Nevertheless, I always make it a point to wake up early to prepare their favourite *tonkatsu* bento on these special days.

Tonkatsu   Serves 4

4 slices pork loin or fillet, each
 about 1-cm ($^1/_2$-inch) thick and
 weighing 150 g ($5^1/_3$ oz)

salt and ground black pepper

70 g ($2^1/_2$ oz) cake flour

1 egg, beaten

80 g ($2^3/_4$ oz) panko breadcrumbs

vegetable oil

shredded cabbage

tonkatsu sauce

1. If using pork loin, make small cuts in the meat using the
 tip of a knife. If using pork fillet, pound lightly. Sprinkle
 salt and pepper on both sides of the meat. Coat with
 flour and pat off the excess. Dip the meat into the
 beaten egg and dredge in the panko.

2. In a deep-frying pan, heat the vegetable oil to 180°C
 (350°F). Deep-fry the meat over medium heat, turning
 once until it is cooked through, and crisp and golden.
 This should take 7–8 minutes. Place on a wire rack to
 drain the excess oil. Serve with shredded cabbage and
 tonkatsu sauce.

Leeks, wonderful with olive oil and ponzu sauce

I was raised in Narashino, on the outskirts of Tokyo, and used to commute to Roppongi, in the centre of Tokyo, when I was a middle school student. In those days, I used to wake up early in the morning, and always enjoyed cycling to the local station, breathing in the fresh air. I felt like I was in some sort of highland resort as I breezed through the huge, verdant vegetable fields. When I got to Roppongi an hour later and started walking with the crowds toward Tokyo Tower, I felt like I was in a totally different world.

Although I left Narashino after getting married, I moved back to my home town, which still contains a lot of farmland, after I had my first child. When my children were small, I loved taking walks with them. They were so proud to tell me the names of the vegetables they saw, such as *ninjin* (carrots) and *negi* (leeks), which they identified by their leaves, repeating in a kind of chant, "*ninjin, ninjin, negi, negi, ninjin, negi.*"

These vegetables are still the area's main crops—in particular the leeks that are carefully grown in soft earth. Baby leeks sprouting in lines always look so pretty to me, reminding me of kindergarteners walking hand-in-hand.

Taking advantage of the ready availability of fresh leeks at the farmers market behind our house, I often make dishes with them.

One such dish is based on my mother's recipe for marinated leeks. She cooks the leeks in soup, leaves the mixture to cool, then pours some olive oil and *ponzu* sauce over them before chilling the dish. The combination of olive oil and *ponzu* may seem unconventional, but it is really tasty. I often cook it as a side dish, adding a few twists to make it more contemporary. It makes an impressive appetizer when you have guests, especially when served with Parma ham or *ikura* (salmon roe).

Leeks with Olive Oil and Ponzu Sauce Serves 4–6

4 leeks

300 ml (1¼ cups) water

1 bouillon cube

2 Tbsp olive oil

ponzu sauce

ikura (salmon roe), for garnish

1. Cut the leeks into 5-cm (2-inch) lengths. Bring the water to a boil in a saucepan. Add the bouillon cube and heat until dissolved. Gently add the leeks and cook covered over low heat for 5–6 minutes until the leeks are tender.

2. In a square container, lay out the leeks in an even layer and cover with 2 Tbsp of the remaining soup from the saucepan. Let cool. Chill in the refrigerator.

3. To serve, arrange the leeks on a serving plate and dress with the olive oil and a little ponzu sauce. Top with *ikura*. Serve.

Pumpkin dessert for a Halloween party

My youngest son brought back an orange envelope from school the other day. In it was an invitation card for a Halloween party from one of his classmates.

Although Halloween is not well understood in Japan, Halloween decorations can be found everywhere during the season. A salesclerk at a store told me that Halloween has become amazingly popular in the last few years, and many young people in particular enjoy Halloween parties without knowing the significance.

When I was little, I knew Halloween only from photographs posted to me by cousins who lived in the United States. I could not imagine what a real jack-o'-lantern was like as I had never seen an orange pumpkin before. I remember that my mother made me a jack-o'-lantern with a watermelon as it was impossible to make one with the thick-rinded Japanese pumpkin.

Nowadays, miniature orange pumpkins are available at many stores along with various kinds of pumpkin-shaped or flavoured cookies, candies and ice creams. I am sure that, as Halloween has made inroads in Japan on a commercial basis, Easter will be celebrated here, too, in the near future.

I have eaten many pumpkin pies in the United States, but I never had the chance to taste pumpkin pudding—now my favourite dessert—or other desserts made from pumpkin. I believe the Japanese *kabocha* is well suited for making pumpkin desserts as it tastes somewhat like chestnuts or sweet potatoes when cooked. It also is bright in colour and dense in texture. Among all my pumpkin recipes, this one for pumpkin pudding is the most popular among my family members.

Make this pudding from fresh pumpkins in season and enhance the taste with high-quality heavy cream.

Pumpkin Pudding

Makes one 18-cm (7-inch) round pudding

Caramel

6 Tbsp sugar

2 Tbsp water

Pudding

butter, for greasing

450 g (1 lb) *kabocha* pumpkin

200 ml ($^5/_6$ cup) milk

200 ml ($^5/_6$ cup) heavy cream

120 g (4 oz) sugar

4 eggs

3 egg yolks

a dash of vanilla extract

1 Tbsp rum

Whipped Cream Topping

200 ml ($^5/_6$ cup) heavy cream

1 Tbsp sugar

1. Lightly butter an 18-cm (7-inch) round mould. Preheat the oven to 170°C (340°F). To make the caramel, put the sugar and water in a small saucepan over low heat until the sugar is completely dissolved and a syrup is formed. Boil the syrup until it begins to turn golden. Swirl the pan over the heat and when the syrup is golden brown, pour it into the mould. Allow to cool.

2. Remove the seeds and spongy parts of the pumpkin. Cut into large chunks and steam for 15–20 minutes or until tender. Remove the skin. Using a food processor, purée the pumpkin until smooth.

3. Scald the milk, heavy cream and sugar in a saucepan over low heat. Remove from the heat and mix well until the sugar is dissolved.

4. In a mixing bowl, beat the eggs and egg yolks. Add the pumpkin purée and mix well. Add the milk mixture, vanilla extract and rum. Strain the mixture into the mould. Place the mould in a deep pan and pour boiling water into the pan to come halfway up the side of the mould. Steam-bake for 40–50 minutes or until the pudding is firm and a toothpick inserted into the centre comes out clean.

5. To unmould the pudding, run a sharp knife around the edge of the pudding. Place a plate over the mould and quickly invert. For the topping, lightly whip the heavy cream with the sugar. Serve the pudding with the cream.

Irresistible stuffed green bell peppers

Whenever we go grocery shopping, my children would always ask me to buy green bell peppers (capsicums). Sometimes they just grab the package of green bell peppers and put it in the shopping cart. Although green bell peppers are supposed to be one of the most unpopular vegetables among children in Japan, my children just love them. When I cook tempura, they fight for the green bell pepper pieces. Grilled or stir-fried green bell peppers is also popular with them. However, when they specifically ask me to buy the vegetable, it means they want me to cook green bell peppers stuffed with minced meat.

To cook the dish, I usually have to buy at least four packs of green bell peppers. Luckily there is a grocery store nearby that often has a *tsumehodai* special bag sale, where you can stuff as many of a certain item as you like into a large plastic bag for a fixed price.

The sale items can be vegetables, such as potatoes, onions or snow peas, or fruits, such as oranges. Whenever green bell peppers are featured, my children would choose the nicest-looking ones and carefully put them into the bag. On one such day, they managed to put 20 large green bell peppers into one bag. Back home, I cut the green bell peppers into halves and made 40 stuffed green bell peppers, but the bell peppers were gone after just a few minutes on the table.

Once, when chicken drumsticks were featured in the bag sale, I observed a man using a refined technique to get the most out of the offer. He carefully stretched the plastic bag and then started placing drumsticks upright in the bag, neatly fitting the wider ends with the narrow ends as if he were putting a puzzle together. After a while, I could see a perfect column of chicken drumsticks in his bag as he began building the second layer. His wife stood beside him without saying anything, watching the procedure intently. The mood was solemn.

I wonder how many chicken drumsticks the man was able to pack into the bag. I wish he had made another pack for me. Having neither the special skills nor enough time to make up such a package, I will continue to let my kids pack their much-loved green bell peppers, so that we can enjoy one of our favourite dishes together.

Stuffed Green Bell Peppers   Serves 4–6

12 green bell peppers (capsicums)

40 g (1¹/₂ oz) panko breadcrumbs

80 ml (¹/₃ cup) milk

¹/₂ onion

450 g (1 lb) minced pork and beef
   mixture

1 egg

²/₃ tsp salt

ground black pepper

1 Tbsp olive oil

ponzu sauce and grated daikon
   radish or sauce of your choice

1. Trim the bell peppers. Cut them in half lengthwise and remove the seeds. Mix the panko with the milk. Peel and mince the onion. In a bowl, combine the minced meat, onion, panko-and-milk mixture and egg. Season with salt and pepper and mix well. Stuff the bell peppers with the meat mixture.

2. Preheat the oven to 180°C (350°F). Place the bell peppers in a large baking pan. Sprinkle olive oil over the bell peppers. Roast for 20–25 minutes until the meat is cooked. The cooking time will depend on the size of the bell peppers.

3. Serve with ponzu sauce and grated daikon, or your favourite sauce.

A great recipe from a school lunch menu

Recently, I joined a programme at my children's elementary school. While the first graders were away on a school excursion, the mothers were invited to taste the school lunches in one of the classrooms. We also received a lecture about how a healthy diet can prevent obesity.

Although it is a public school, it is fitted with a very modern kitchen, and the schoolchildren seem happy with the wonderful warm lunches prepared using high quality foodstuff, including locally grown vegetables in season.

The menu for the tasting party consisted of some of the most popular dishes among the children—kimchi *chahan* (kimchi fried rice), teriyaki-style crispy fried squid, cucumber and bean sprout salad and clear vegetable soup with bamboo shoots and wakame seaweed. At the school, 60 kg (130 lb) of rice is cooked each time for the 940 students, which includes the children at a kindergarten occupying the same premises. Although *chahan* means fried rice, the dish is cooked in huge rice cookers, since it is almost impossible to cook nearly a thousand servings of fried rice using woks.

At the school, a milder version of kimchi *chahan* is made for the younger children and a spicier one for the older students, enabling everybody from the kindergarteners to the sixth graders to enjoy the same menu.

I enjoyed the *chahan* and recreated the dish at home. It is very quick to prepare and my children were happy to get their favourite school lunch at home. I realized it was a good idea to cook the dish with a rice cooker as cooking a huge portion of fried rice in a wok is tiring work.

VARIATION This recipe uses dried shiitake mushrooms, but you can use fresh ones as well. If using fresh shiitake mushrooms, you may need to add extra water to the cup containing the kimchi liquid and the juices of the stir-fried vegetables and meat.

Kimchi Fried Rice   Serves 4

3 dried shiitake mushrooms

160 ml (^{2}/$_3$ cup) warm water

480 g (17 oz) uncooked Japanese rice

100 g (3^1/$_2$ oz) Chinese cabbage kimchi

200 g (7 oz) pork or chicken

1 tsp + 2 Tbsp Japanese soy sauce

1 tsp + 1 Tbsp sake

1 carrot

1 tsp vegetable oil

1 Tbsp mirin

1 tsp salt

480 ml (2 cups) water

1 tsp sesame oil

1. Briefly wash the shiitake, then soak in the 160 ml (^{2}/$_3$ cup) warm water for 1–2 hours, or overnight for the best flavour. If possible, keep the stalks pointing downward while soaking. (If you are in a hurry, you can place the shiitake and water in the microwave oven for 2 minutes and let the shiitake soak in the water until the water cools.) When the shiitake are soft, remove from the water, reserving the water, and gently squeeze with fingers. Discard the stems of the shiitake and chop the caps into small chunks.

2. Rinse the rice until the water becomes clear, then drain. Drain the kimchi, reserving the liquid in a small cup. Cut the kimchi into 1-cm (1/2-inch) pieces. Cut the meat into 1-cm (1/2-inch) cubes and sprinkle with 1 tsp soy sauce and 1 tsp sake. Peel and chop the carrot into small chunks. In a frying pan, heat the vegetable oil and stir-fry the carrot, meat and shiitake. Add 2 Tbsp soy sauce, 1 Tbsp sake, mirin and salt and cook until heated through. Drain the cooking juices and reserve.

3. In a cup, mix the reserved kimchi liquid, shiitake soaking water and cooking juices of the stir-fried vegetables and meat. Top up with water to make 240 ml (1 cup) of liquid. Cook the rice following the instructions on page 126, using this cup of liquid and the 480 ml (2 cups) of water. When the rice is cooked, mix it with the kimchi, stir-fried vegetables and meat and sesame oil. Serve.

Magical pumpkin, a versatile vegetable

The days are getting shorter and shorter as the winter solstice nears. In Japan, we have a custom of taking a yuzu citrus bath and eating a particular food on the day of the solstice—pumpkin.

In ancient times, pumpkin was considered very nutritious. Eating pumpkin was believed to prevent serious diseases. It also was believed that eating pumpkin on the day of the winter solstice would ensure protection from evil spirits. Since it must have been difficult to get fresh vegetables during the winter in those days, it is no wonder that the vitamin-rich pumpkin, which keeps long after harvesting, was regarded as a precious vegetable.

For breakfast, my kids often say, "*Are tabetai* (I want to eat that)." "That" refers to my special pumpkin balls which I always keep stock of in the freezer. When I have the time, I usually steam a whole pumpkin. I use the vegetable's green skin to make green potage soup and mash the rest of the vegetable with stir-fried chicken and onion to make pumpkin balls the size of golf balls.

It is very helpful to have these pumpkin balls in the freezer. When you do not have enough time to cook, you can put some of the balls in a casserole and microwave them for a few minutes before topping them with cheese and baking in the oven until the cheese becomes lightly browned. For an even tastier dish, cover the balls with tomato sauce or white sauce and top with cheese. Or dust the pumpkin balls with cake flour, dip them in beaten egg and coat with breadcrumbs before deep-frying until golden to make tasty pumpkin croquettes. When a friend visited me with her baby, the pumpkin balls also proved to be a perfect baby food.

To serve the pumpkin balls for breakfast as a side dish, I microwave them on a plate, put each ball in a heatproof silicon or aluminium cup, sprinkle cheese over, then bake them for few minutes in an oven toaster. This baked pumpkin ball is useful for filling my children's lunch boxes too.

For me, pumpkin is a magic vegetable—not just during the winter solstice, but every day of the year.

Pumpkin Balls   Makes about 30 balls

900 g (2 lb) *kabocha* pumpkin
1 onion
10 g (¹/₃ oz) butter
200 g (7 oz) minced chicken
salt and ground black pepper

1. Cut the pumpkin into chunks and remove the seeds and spongy parts. Steam for 30 minutes or until tender. Remove the peel and mash the flesh in a large bowl. A food processor can be used.

2. Peel and chop the onion. In a frying pan, heat the butter and cook the onion over medium heat until semi-transparent. Add the chicken, season with salt and pepper and cook until heated through. Remove from the heat and add the chicken mixture to the mashed pumpkin. Let the mixture cool, then refrigerate for 2–3 hours until completely chilled and firm.

3. Using your hands, make balls the size of golf balls with the mixture. Place the balls on a flat tray lined with waxed paper and freeze. Once frozen, put the balls in a plastic bag and store in the freezer until needed.

Japanese mayonnaise, the key to good potato salad

At this time last year, my German friend, Monika, visited me for two weeks. It was her fourth trip to Japan since she first came for my university graduation ceremony about 20 years ago. Then, three years later, she came to attend my wedding. She is very good at baking, and we baked two kinds of German cake back then to serve at the wedding reception. It took a lot of time to bake for more than a hundred guests, but it became our wonderful shared memory.

When she visited me the third time, I was on maternity leave after having my first child. After that, we were too busy to visit each other as she had a job and I had four children to take care of. Her visit last year was thus the first in a long time.

Monika loves Japanese food and enjoys eating the many kinds of dishes that I cook, often asking me for the recipes so she can prepare them for herself back home. Among the dishes is my potato salad, which she says is special for being so succulent. When she asked me in a letter how to prepare it some years ago, I realized I had no particular recipe for the dish as I usually combine ingredients that vary according to my mood on the day. Even so, I soon wrote out the recipe and sent it to her. However, she wrote back to inform me that when she tried to prepare the dish with ingredients available in Germany, it did not turn out well.

When she visited me last year, she baked a huge *linzer torte,* one of the cakes we had baked for the wedding reception. And we also finally figured out that the mayonnaise was the key to success with the potato salad. Monika could not reproduce my potato salad because Japanese mayonnaise was not available in Germany.

Of course, she took some Japanese mayonnaise back with her, and said she planned to treat her friends to the perfect potato salad. Now I'm sure that she will have to visit me again sometime in the near future to get another tube of her favourite mayonnaise!

Potato Salad   Serves 4–6

1 cucumber
salt, as needed
¹/₂ onion
6 slices ham
2 hard-boiled eggs
¹/₂ carrot
4 potatoes
1 Tbsp vinegar
6 Tbsp Japanese mayonnaise
ground black pepper

1. Slice the cucumber into thin rounds. Sprinkle with salt, leave for 5 minutes, then lightly squeeze in a paper towel to remove excess moisture.

2. Peel and slice the onion very thinly, then leave in a bowl of cold water. Cut the ham into small pieces. Peel and roughly chop the hard-boiled eggs.

3. Peel the carrot and cut into 5-mm (¹/₄-inch) thick fan-shaped slices. Boil the carrot slices for 3–4 minutes, then drain.

4. Peel and cut the potatoes into small pieces, then boil until tender. Drain and roughly mash while hot. Add the vinegar to the mashed potato and mix. Drain and squeeze excess water from the onion and add to the mashed potato. Let the mixture cool until lukewarm. Add the carrot, ham, egg, mayonnaise, ¹/₄ tsp salt and pepper and mix. When the salad has cooled completely, mix in the cucumber. Serve.

Handy hashiyasume for a special occasion

Merry Christmas! Are you planning to have a special dinner tonight? I am almost too tired to prepare dinner and presents for my four children. As the younger boys still believe in Santa Claus, the elder children are trying to take advantage of this in order to get something from 'Santa' themselves.

When I think about the menu for a special dinner, it is quite easy to decide what to cook as the main dish because in most cases, it will be something with meat. So, I usually try to prepare some seafood as a side dish. Marinated salmon with cucumber dressing, an original recipe of my grandmother's, is a very convenient dish as you can prepare it a couple of days in advance and keep it in the refrigerator.

My grandmother often told me the story of how she created this recipe when she was young. One day nearly 50 years ago, when my grandmother was spending the summer in her vacation house by a lake, her sister dropped in unannounced at lunch time with other guests. Her sister, a culinary expert who owned a cooking school, told my grandmother that the others were gourmets. This upset my grandmother as she had nothing special on hand to serve to these guests.

Still, she had fresh rainbow trout from the lake and cucumbers from the field. She decided to sauté the fish. While preparing the fish, she thought of adding grated cucumber to the regular dressing, and it turned out to be wonderfully tasty. She served the sautéed fish with the green cucumber dressing to the guests and everybody was quite pleased with her creation. She proudly told me that the recipe was eventually published in a magazine.

Later, she combined the cucumber dressing with steamed salmon and often served the dish as *hashiyasume*—a dish that contrasts in flavour and texture to the main side dish. I prefer the latter, as the combination of pink salmon and green cucumber looks so inviting.

The recipe goes well with Western and Japanese dishes. The dish can be served as an antipasto or as a salad if you add more vegetables. Deep-fried fish such as tiny *aji* (horse mackerel) or boiled prawns (shrimp), squid, octopus or scallops are also good to serve with the dressing.

Marinated Salmon with Cucumber Dressing   Serves 6

1 medium onion

6 salmon fillets

100 ml (²/₅ cup) sake

a pinch of salt

100 ml (²/₅ cup) vegetable oil

100 ml (²/₅ cup) vinegar

1 tsp salt

1 Tbsp sugar

ground white pepper, to taste

1¹/₂ cucumbers

1. Peel the onion, slice thinly and leave in a bowl of water.

2. Cut each salmon fillet into 4 pieces and place in a large frying pan in a single layer. Sprinkle the salmon with sake and salt, then cook, covered, over low heat for 7–8 minutes or until cooked through.

3. To make the dressing, combine the vegetable oil, vinegar, salt, sugar and pepper in a bowl and whisk. Cut off the ends of the cucumber and grate. Add the grated cucumber to the dressing and mix well.

4. Drain the onion slices. In a flat-bottom container, place the salmon and the drained onion slices and pour the cucumber dressing over the top. Allow to marinate for at least 2–3 hours before serving. The marinated salmon will keep for 2–3 days in the refrigerator.

Big Bowls
of Mother's Love

Great ideas for using strawberries

Strawberries are in season. Behind our house, a farmers market is held every weekend, while a strawberry stall opens three times a week during the season.

When I was little, a neighbouring farming couple used to grow vegetables such as onions, carrots and cucumbers. Sometimes in the summer, they also planted watermelons, probably just for themselves to enjoy. As my mother used to buy fresh vegetables from them, they would sometimes give us watermelons as a gift. At times, there would be more watermelons than we could eat and we would enjoy a traditional Japanese game called *suikawari* (watermelon splitting) with friends.

After many years, the fieldwork was taken over by the couple's son and his wife. About seven years ago, they dug a well and started building greenhouses. The first year, they grew asparagus. Then they increased the number of greenhouses and started growing strawberries as a side business.

I was very surprised as I had never imagined strawberries growing in our neighbourhood just outside Tokyo. The older lady proudly informed me that it was her grandson's idea. I had seen the young man working with great diligence in the greenhouses.

The side business quickly became successful. During the first year, the young man had asked my daughter to draw a picture of strawberries to be used on a signboard for their strawberry stall. When her drawing was done, the young man gave her boxes of beautiful strawberries and, thanks to him, we were able to make a wonderful strawberry shortcake for my daughter's birthday party that November. We also enjoyed *ichigogari* (strawberry picking) at their greenhouse the following year during the Golden Week holiday period at the beginning of May, which is the end of the strawberry season.

With the greenhouses, my neighbours are now able to supply the stall with fresh strawberries throughout the season.

Yoghurt bavarois made with strawberries is my favourite quick dessert. For this recipe, I recommend using small strawberries sold for jam-making at reasonable prices.

VARIATION For a low-calorie alternative, omit the heavy cream and increase the quantities of milk and yoghurt to 300 ml (1¼ cups) each to make strawberry yoghurt jelly.

Strawberry Yoghurt Bavarois   Serves 8

15 g (¹/₂ oz) gelatin powder
6 Tbsp water
300 g (10¹/₂ oz) strawberries
1 tsp lemon juice
180 ml (³/₄ cup) milk
150 g (5¹/₄ oz) sugar
180 ml (³/₄ cup) heavy cream
240 ml (1 cup) plain yoghurt

1. Soak the gelatin in the water. Wash and hull the strawberries, then drain. In a bowl, mash the strawberries with a fork and sprinkle with the lemon juice.

2. In a saucepan, scald the milk and add the sugar and the gelatin-and-water mixture. Stir gently until the sugar and gelatin dissolve. Let cool.

3. In a bowl, beat the heavy cream until soft peaks form. Add the mashed strawberries and stir well. Add the yoghurt and gently stir. Add the milk, sugar and gelatin mixture. Pour into a large mould or several smaller individual moulds. Chill in the refrigerator until set.

A big bowl of mother's love

Spring vacation is over and a new school year has started. School lunches have finally started to free me from cooking three times a day for my children. Although I usually enjoy cooking, there are times when I feel like I don't even want to think about it, especially when it comes to dinner or when I'm too exhausted. At such times and when I want to save time and energy, I often cook *donburi,* individual bowls of rice served with various toppings.

There are many types of *donburi* and they include *oyako donburi* (chicken and egg on rice), *katsudon* (pork cutlet on rice) and *tendon* (tempura on rice), but one of my favourite dishes to cook is *sanshoku* (three-colour) *donburi*, a bowl of rice topped with *iritamago* (scrambled egg), *torisoboro* (minced chicken) and spinach.

The combination of these three toppings is also a popular menu for children's bento boxes. When I was little, my mother often made a *sanshoku* bento for me to take to kindergarten. Honestly speaking, I would have loved it if she had stuck to a *nishoku* (two-colour) bento, which does not come with green vegetables. However, my mother determinedly added either stir-fried spinach or boiled peas to my bento box.

As a mother myself, now I understand why she always put green vegetables between the yellow *iritamago* and beige *torisoboro*, as they make the meal look much tastier. Besides, there has to be some vegetables for the sake of balanced nutrition.

For me, the green vegetables on a *sanshokudon* are the symbol of a mother's conscience. There is a hidden message from mothers in the dish—that they tried their best to cook a balanced meal for their family even though they were tired or did not want to cook some time-consuming dish. (*Donburi* also leaves fewer dishes to wash afterward, another good excuse for making it.)

Sanshokudon has protein, carbohydrates, vitamins and fibre as well as a mother's love and sense of responsibility.

For these reasons, I recommend that you serve this ultimate *donburi* for dinner. Should you have extra energy or want to show even more of your affection, you may serve some soup on the side.

Sanshoku Donburi   Serves 4

salt and ground black pepper

200 g (7 oz) spinach

1 tsp vegetable oil

toasted white sesame seeds,
  for garnish

4 *donburi* bowls, about two-thirds
  filled with cooked Japanese rice
  (page 126)

Iritamago

4 eggs

$1/4$ tsp salt

1 tsp sugar

1 tsp vegetable oil

Torisoboro

1 tsp vegetable oil

300 g ($10^1/_2$ oz) minced chicken

1 tsp grated fresh ginger

2 Tbsp Japanese soy sauce

2 Tbsp mirin

1 Tbsp sake

1 Tbsp cornflour (cornstarch)
  or $1/_2$ Tbsp *katakuriko*

1 Tbsp water

1. Prepare the spinach. Boil a pot of water and add a pinch
   of salt. Add the spinach and parboil for 1 minute. Drain
   and immerse in cold water to cool and seal the colour.
   Gather the stem ends together and squeeze out the water
   by hand. Cut off and discard the stems. Cut the leaves
   into 2.5-cm (1-inch) lengths. Set aside.

2. To make the *iritamago*, beat the eggs in a bowl with salt
   and sugar. In a frying pan, heat the oil and cook the egg
   over medium-low heat, stirring constantly with chopsticks
   until it is almost set. Remove from the heat and keep
   stirring until the egg is finely crumbled. (For fine-grained
   iritamago, I stir with 2 pairs of chopsticks held together.
   You can use a fork, but be careful not to scratch the pan.)

3. To make the *torisoboro,* heat the vegetable oil in a clean
   frying pan. Add the minced chicken and stir-fry over
   medium heat. Add the grated ginger, soy sauce, mirin
   and sake. Cook for 2–3 minutes, stirring constantly,
   until heated through. In a small cup, mix the cornflour or
   katakuriko and 1 Tbsp water. Add to the chicken mixture
   and stir to thicken the sauce. Remove from the heat.

4. In a clean frying pan, heat the vegetable oil and stir-fry the
   spinach. Lightly season with salt and pepper and sprinkle
   with sesame seeds.

5. Arrange the *iritamago*, *torisoboro* and spinach on top of
   the rice in each *donburi* bowl. Serve.

A taste of Taiwan

During the spring vacation, my three sons and I joined a church group for a trip to Taiwan. Although it was only for four days, we enjoyed our stay. The first day, my two younger children and I somehow missed lunch and the boys were starving by dinnertime. When we arrived at the restaurant for dinner, I saw a signboard that read Restaurant Frogs. My first impression was that "frogs" did not mean anything other than being the restaurant's name, but there was a large water tank in front of the entrance, in which big frogs were swimming!

When the first dish came, I soon realized it was deep-fried frog legs. The fried frog legs were piled up high on the huge plate and I was afraid that my younger boys might get shocked or scream when they realized what they were. However, they were too hungry to be surprised. They loved the dish and just kept asking me for more. My youngest son, who had piled his plate high with frog bones, even asked me to cook fried frogs for him when we got back to Japan. He also promised me that he would help by catching the frogs himself.

Well, it isn't possible for me to cook frog legs in Japan, but I learnt some other tasty recipes from the mother of our host family in Taiwan. One of the dishes was stir-fried prawns (shrimp) and *nagaimo* (yam) wrapped with lettuce leaves. Before serving the dish for lunch, she broke some Chinese fried bread sticks—left over from our breakfast, which also included other dishes—into small pieces and sprinkled them over the prawns and *nagaimo*. The combination of ingredients was just great.

As soon as I came home to Japan, I cooked it for dinner. Although Chinese fried bread sticks are available frozen at a Chinese grocery store here, I tried a substitute ingredient in the form of deep-fried spring roll wrappers. It turned out quite tasty. If you can't get hold of *nagaimo*, *renkon* (lotus root) or *takenoko* (bamboo shoots) will also yield tasty results.

Stir-fried Prawns and Nagaimo with Lettuce   Serves 4

450 g (1 lb) prawns (shrimp)

1 tsp Japanese soy sauce

1 tsp sake

200 g (7 oz) *nagaimo* (yam)

vegetable oil as needed

$^{1}/_{3}$ tsp salt

80 ml ($^{1}/_{3}$ cup) chicken stock

2 Tbsp cornflour (cornstarch)
  or 1 Tbsp *katakuriko*

2 Tbsp water

4 spring roll wrappers
  (or 1 Chinese fried bread stick)

1 medium head lettuce

1. Peel the prawns and remove the tails. Devein by inserting a toothpick into the back of each prawn and gently removing the thin black line. Coarsely chop the prawns and sprinkle with the soy sauce and sake.

2. Peel the *nagaimo* and cut into 5-mm ($^{1}/_{2}$-inch) cubes.

3. In a frying pan, heat 1 tsp vegetable oil over high heat. Add the prawns and stir-fry until the colour changes. Add the *nagaimo* and salt and cook for 2 minutes. Add the chicken stock and stir.

4. In a small cup, quickly mix the cornflour with the 2 Tbsp water. When the ingredients in the pan start to boil, stir in the cornflour mixture. Cook while stirring until the liquid becomes thick. Remove from the heat.

5. In a deep frying pan, heat enough vegetable oil for deep-frying to 170°C (340°F). Deep-fry the spring roll wrappers one by one until crisp and golden. Drain.

6. Just before serving, break the fried spring roll wrappers (or Chinese fried bread stick) into small pieces and add to the stir-fried prawns and *nagaimo* mixture. Serve with the lettuce leaves.

Time to enjoy the fresh taste of spring veggies

Here comes the season where you can find many seasonal vegetables in the markets, including various kinds of buds and sprouts. Young bamboo shoots and other edible wild plants have a special prominence at this time of the year.

In spring, it takes a long time for me to decide which vegetable to buy. But my appetite is always whetted by anything with the words *haru* (spring) or *shin* (new) in the name—a sign that they are the harvest of this season. *Haru kyabetsu* (spring cabbage) and *shin tamanegi* (newly harvested onions), for example, just sound great, and always go straight into my shopping basket.

Spring cabbage is a vegetable I love to cook. It is tender and juicy compared to regular cabbage as it contains lots of water. The outer leaves are a bright green colour, while the inner leaves are yellowish and somewhat sweet. The texture goes well with many other seasonal ingredients, and, most importantly, it is not expensive.

I like to stir-fry spring cabbage with thinly sliced beef and season it simply with salt, pepper and a little bit of soy sauce or oyster sauce. I also like to cook the cabbage with bacon or sausage—a nice combination that can be included in pasta dishes, soups or salads. But one of my favourite dinner recipes for the vegetable is a simple dish with sautéed salmon, served with a creamy sour sauce.

I used to serve sautéed salmon with mayonnaise and lemon juice or with tartar sauce. But once, when I ran out of mayonnaise, I used some heavy cream which I had in the refrigerator instead. After cooking the salmon and removing it from the frying pan, I added the heavy cream with some soy sauce and lemon juice. The mixture became a beige-coloured creamy sour sauce which tasted quite good. I also found that the sauce goes well with sautéed mushrooms.

With the sautéed salmon dish, everybody eats a lot of cabbage. Although some of my children do not like eating the hard parts of regular cabbage, they love to eat spring cabbage as even the harder parts are still tender and tasty.

Sautéed Salmon with Spring Cabbage   Serves 4

$^1/_2$ head spring cabbage

2 Tbsp vegetable oil

salt and ground white pepper

4 servings salmon fillet

1 Tbsp cake flour

6 Tbsp heavy cream

2 tsp Japanese soy sauce

1 tsp lemon juice

1. Cut the cabbage into wedges and then into chunks. In a frying pan, heat 1 Tbsp vegetable oil and stir-fry the cabbage over high heat for 3–4 minutes until cooked but still crisp. Lightly season with salt and pepper and set aside.

2. Drain the salmon fillets on paper towels. Lightly season with salt and pepper and dust with the cake flour. In a clean frying pan, heat the other tablespoon of vegetable oil over medium heat. Cook the salmon fillets in the oil for 1 minute and then turn over. Reduce the heat to low and cook covered for 4–5 minutes until heated through. Remove from the heat and place on individual serving plates with the stir-fried cabbage.

3. Using the same pan, add the heavy cream and soy sauce and stir gently over low heat for about 30 seconds. Before the mixture starts boiling, remove from the heat and mix in the lemon juice. Pour the sauce over the salmon and serve.

A dish to satisfy the biggest appetite

In April, my eldest son, who is 14, started his third year of middle school. He has grown so much during the last two years, and is now is 20 cm (8 inches) taller than when he first entered the school. Of course, he eats a lot, and I feel like his large bento box is bottomless whenever I try to pack it with food for him.

Recently, he invited two of his friends home. I decided to cook a voluminous lunch for them—huge plates of lasagne and salad and a basketful of bread. In no time at all, they finished the lot, even though I had thought it would be too much.

The trio then spent the whole afternoon playing together, having snacks from time to time. Later, my son told me that one of his friends had decided to stay with us for dinner. I had not made any particular preparations for dinner that day as I had thought there would be enough leftover lasagne from lunch. However, when I opened the refrigerator, I came up with the idea of cooking *wafu loco moco*, my son's favourite dish. *Wafu* means Japanese-style and this recipe adds a soy sauce-based sauce and garnishes of daikon radish and shiso leaves to the popular Hawaiian burger-and-egg-over-rice concoction. I usually cook the dish with small hamburger patties I stock in the freezer for bento boxes.

I served the dish to the boys for dinner in the largest *donburi* rice bowls I had. They were very pleased. When my son's friend finished the food, I asked him, just to be polite, if it was enough for him (as I believed the portion was definitely large enough). He smiled and replied, "Sure, I'm all right as I make it a rule to eat another *donburi* before going to bed." I managed a smile and said, "That's a good idea." At that moment, I could only envy the incredible appetite of the teenager.

Wafu Loco Moco   Serves 4

1 Tbsp vegetable oil

4 hamburger patties

$^1/_8$ head cabbage

1 avocado

1 tomato

5-cm (2-inch) length daikon radish

3 shiso leaves

1 knob fresh ginger

3 Tbsp Japanese soy sauce

3 Tbsp mirin

4 eggs

4 *donburi* bowls, about two-thirds filled with cooked Japanese rice (page 126)

shichimi togarashi

1. In a frying pan, heat the vegetable oil over medium-high heat and add the hamburger patties. Cook for 1 minute and turn the patties over. Turn the heat to low and cook covered for 7–8 minutes until the patties are heated through. Test for doneness by inserting a toothpick into the patties. If the juices run clear, the patties are ready.

2. Discard the hard part of the cabbage and shred the leaves. Cut the avocado into slices about 1-cm ($^1/_2$-inch) thick. Cut the tomato into wedges. Peel and grate the daikon and drain. Shred the shiso leaves.

3. To make the sauce, peel and grate the ginger and combine it with the soy sauce and mirin. Heat in a frying pan over medium heat. When the sauce starts boiling, turn off the heat.

4. Prepare 4 sunny-side up fried eggs. Cover each *donburi* bowl of rice with cabbage. Arrange the patties, avocado and tomato on top of the cabbage. Top with a sunny-side up egg, grated daikon and shiso leaves. Pour the sauce over the top and sprinkle with *shichimi togarashi*. Serve.

Korean pancakes for a rainy day

Kuniko, a Japanese friend of mine who lives in Seoul, sent me an e-mail during the rainy season last year and told me an interesting story about *pajon* (Korean pancakes) she'd heard. She was told that South Koreans especially like to eat *pajon* on rainy days. When she asked some South Korean friends for a reason, the explanations varied.

"Rainy weather makes people feel depressed, so they like to get together and cook *pajon*," one friend told her.

"When it's raining, you don't feel like going grocery shopping, but you'll always find the ingredients for *pajon* in your pantry," another friend explained.

"The crispy texture of *pajon* stimulates the appetite and makes people feel revitalized," a third said.

Kuniko also told me that she did not know what to say when she was asked what the special food for rainy days was in Japan. We don't seem to have any special meal to enjoy on a rainy day. But it must be wonderful to get together with friends and cook with an electric hot plate, especially during the annoying rainy season when you can get depressed, lose your appetite or feel too lazy to cook more complex dishes.

Kuniko gave me a tasty recipe for *pajon* with squid and garlic chives she learned at a cooking class she attended in Korea. In her recipe, she recommends using tempura flour. Although I had some *pajon* flour at home, I tried using tempura flour, and it made very light and crispy *pajon*. You can also cook *pajon* by combining cake flour and cornflour (cornstarch).

PREPARING SQUID Unless you are used to preparing squid yourself, I recommend using prepared frozen squid. Be sure to cut it while it is semi-frozen, as it is easier to handle then.

SUBSTITUTE FOR FLOUR If you can get hold of it, tempura flour also works well in this recipe. Substitute the cake flour and cornflour with 250 g (9 oz) tempura flour.

Pajon with Squid and Garlic Chives   Makes 4 large *pajon*

140 g (5 oz) prepared squid

100 g (3¹/₂ oz) garlic chives

1 fresh red chilli

1 fresh green chilli

200 g (7 oz) cake flour

50 g (1³/₄ oz) cornflour (cornstarch)
   or *katakuriko*

400 ml (1²/₃ cups) water

4 Tbsp vegetable oil

Dipping Sauce

3 Tbsp Japanese soy sauce

1 Tbsp sesame oil

¹/₂ Tbsp ground toasted
   white sesame seeds

¹/₂ Tbsp chopped spring onion

¹/₂ Tbsp dried chilli flakes

¹/₂ Tbsp mirin

1. Cut the squid into 1-cm (¹/₂-inch) square pieces. Cut the garlic chives into 2-cm (³/₄-inch) long sections. Slice the fresh green and red chillies into halves lengthwise, remove seeds and cut into slivers.

2. Sift the cake flour and cornflour together in a bowl. Add the water to make a batter. Add the squid, garlic chives and chillies.

3. In a frying pan, heat 1 Tbsp vegetable oil over medium heat. Pour in a ladleful of the mixture so that it spreads thinly in a round shape in the frying pan. Cook for about 2 minutes and turn the pancake over. Cook for another 2 minutes or until the pancake is heated through and crispy. Remove from the pan and set aside. Repeat this process until all the mixture is used up.

4. In a cup, combine the ingredients for the dipping sauce and stir.

5. Serve the *pajon* with the dipping sauce.

Somen noodles for the summer

During the summer vacation, I often serve *somen* for lunch. One of the reasons I like *somen* is that it takes a very short time to cook and I don't have to spend too long in the kitchen. Although I usually lose my appetite in the humid summer, cold *somen* served with cucumber, ham, sliced egg crêpe (see recipe on page 87) or boiled chicken, and topped with condiments, such as grated ginger or shredded shiso leaves, always stimulates my appetite and I often end up eating much more than the children.

The other day, I sent my eight-year-old son to the grocery store to get some packs of *somen* for a weekend lunch. I showed him the packaging of my favourite brand and instructed him to buy that particular brand. After a while, he returned with a packet of noodles I had never seen before. He explained that he had chosen the packet of *somen* for its name, No. 1 Somen, which sounded quite impressive to him. Then, pointing to the copy on the packet, he said, "Mom, I chose it because it says *Sara*

ni koshi ga tsuyoku. (Now with an even stronger bite.) He said he thought it would be good for my back as I complain about back pain. "If you eat this *somen*, your back will become stronger, right?" he said.

He had mistaken the Japanese word *koshi* to mean back as the word also has this meaning. Of course, I gave him a big hug and explained that *koshi* referred to the texture of the noodles in this context.

Nevertheless, he was very happy to eat his favourite tomato *somen* once it was ready. As for me, I could not stop laughing as I held the packet of No. 1 Somen in my hand. The Japanese language is indeed difficult to comprehend.

PREPARED EEL Ready-grilled *unagi kabayaki* complete with *kabayaki no tare* sauce can be found in the freezer section of Asian grocery stores.

MENTSUYU Instant *mentsuyu* is available at Asian grocery stores. Prepare according to the manufacturer's directions. Alternatively, make your own *mentsuyu* with the recipe provided here.

Somen Topped with Tomato and Unagi   Serves 4

1 *unagi kabayaki* (ready-grilled eel fillet)

16–20 cherry tomatoes, trimmed

2 medium shiso leaves

400 g (14 oz) *somen* noodles

240 ml (1 cup) cold water

1 Tbsp toasted white sesame seeds

ice cubes

Mentsuyu Dipping Sauce

10 g (¹/₃ oz) dried konbu, about 15 x 5 cm (2 x 6 inch)

800 ml (3¹/₃ cups) water

180 ml (³/₄ cup) Japanese soy sauce

180 ml (³/₄ cup) mirin

20 g (²/₃ oz) bonito flakes

1. Prepare the *mentsuyu* dipping sauce. Soak the konbu in the water for 30 minutes. Add the soy sauce and mirin and bring to a boil. Add the bonito flakes and simmer for 2–3 minutes, stirring occasionally. Turn off the heat and allow to cool. Strain sauce. This sauce will keep for 3–4 days in the refrigerator.

2. Cut the *unagi* into halves lengthwise, then cut the halves into 1-cm (¹/₂-inch) wide pieces. Cover with plastic wrap and heat in the microwave for 30 seconds or until slightly warm. Allow to cool.

3. Halve the tomatoes. Cut the shiso leaves into halves lengthwise and shred.

4. Bring a large pot of water to a boil and add the *somen* noodles. Cook for 1–2 minutes over medium heat, stirring constantly to keep the noodles separate. When the water is about to boil again, add the cup of cold water. When it returns to a boil, remove the pan from the heat and drain the noodles.

5. To serve, divide the *somen* among 4 individual serving bowls. Gently pour in the cold *mentsuyu*. Top with *unagi*, tomato and shiso leaves. Sprinkle the toasted sesame seeds on the noodles and arrange some ice cubes over the top to keep the dish cool.

Chilled chicken meatballs, a healthy diet recipe?

When I first heard of metabolic syndrome, I had no idea what it meant. However, as the concept became familiar to me, I gradually started to worry about my husband.

When I first met him, he was in his 20s and already carrying an extra kilo or two. This it didn't seem strange to me when, little by little, he gained weight after we were married.

I don't like men who complain about the food they are served or who have unhealthy dietary habits. In these aspects, my husband is perfect. He enjoys dinner with our children even when he's having a whisky. (Some Japanese men do not have a decent meal until they finish drinking.) He does not complain about the food and finishes everything on the table. When I serve fruit after dinner or enjoy a piece of cake or some ice cream at night, he happily tucks into that too.

But the consequence of being such an obliging eater is that he has started to gain weight. To help him lose weight, I started to cook dishes that are low in calories. This dish of chilled meatballs made of minced chicken and tofu is one of my healthy summer diet recipes which uses no oil.

When preparing this dish, you can also make soup with the resulting stock. Skim off the surplus fat that is rendered from the chicken when boiling the meatballs and add vegetables, salt, pepper and soy sauce or *nam pla* (Thai fish sauce) to the stock for a tasty soup. (A favourite with my children is tomato and egg soup prepared with a dash of *kurozu* or black vinegar.)

I recommend serving the chicken and tofu meatballs with vegetables and a dipping sauce as the meatballs taste very plain and light on their own. But lay on various kinds of dipping sauces and it becomes very difficult to stop eating the meatballs. I always end up having too many and I'm not sure if I can call this a diet recipe after all.

Instead of boiling them, you can also deep-fry the chicken and tofu meatballs or cook them as you would regular hamburger patties, and season them with teriyaki sauce.

DIPPING SAUCES Recipes for an *umeboshi-nam pla* dipping sauce and a sesame dipping sauce are provided here, but ponzu and other store-bought sauces are also good options for dipping sauces.

Chilled Chicken and Tofu Meatballs   Makes about 20 meatballs

Meatballs

1 leek

1 knob fresh ginger

140 g (5 oz) block soft tofu, drained
(see Note on page 14)

450 g (1 lb) minced chicken

1 egg

2 Tbsp cornflour (cornstarch)
or *katakuriko*

½ tsp salt

1 tsp Japanese soy sauce

1 tsp mirin

shiso leaves or shredded cucumber

Umeboshi-Nam Pla Dipping Sauce

1 *umeboshi*

1 Tbsp Thai fish sauce (*nam pla*)

1 Tbsp mirin

Sesame Dipping Sauce

1 Tbsp sesame paste

1 Tbsp Japanese soy sauce

1 Tbsp mayonnaise

1. Chop the leek finely. Peel and grate the ginger. Place the leek and ginger in a mixing bowl with the rest of the ingredients for the meatballs and mix well.

2. Bring a pot of water to a boil. Scoop up a ball of the meat mixture with a tablespoon and use another tablespoon to scrape the meatball gently from the first spoon to shape the mixture, then drop it into the boiling water. Repeat the process until the meatball mixture is used up. When the meatballs float to the surface, scoop them up with a perforated ladle and drain. Let them cool to near room temperature, then chill them in the refrigerator. Serve the chilled meatballs with shiso leaves or shredded cucumber and the dipping sauces.

3. To make the *umeboshi-nam pla* dipping sauce, remove the pit from the *umeboshi* and mash the flesh into a paste with a fork. Combine with the *nam pla* and the mirin.

4. To make the sesame dipping sauce, combine all the ingredients and mix well.

Handy and tasty simmered pork

What do you wish you had in your refrigerator when you are too busy to go grocery shopping or are unable to find the time to cook dinner for your hungry children? I would definitely like to have a simmered slab of pork. With that in the refrigerator, I know I have nothing to worry about—even if I'm out and only returning home late in the evening.

I usually make this dish with a 900-g (2-lb) cut of pork shoulder. It is a very simple recipe. You just have to boil the meat for an hour with water, sake, soy sauce, mirin and sugar, along with the green part of a spring onion and sliced ginger, occasionally skimming off any fat and foam. The result is tasty, golden, simmered pork.

I serve the simmered pork with fresh vegetables such as shredded cucumber or lettuce leaves. I also like to cook vegetables, such as ladies fingers (okra) or bok choy, in the remaining stock, and serve them with the meat. You can also make a tasty brown-coloured boiled egg by just soaking a pre-boiled egg in the sauce overnight. (If you do not have time to soak the egg overnight, just simmer it in the sauce for half an hour.) My children also like to eat *donburi* topped with this sliced simmered pork, some vegetables and a boiled egg.

Slices of the simmered pork can also be served with *ramen* or *hiyashi chuka* (cold Chinese noodles with egg, cucumber and other toppings). When diced, the simmered pork makes a great ingredient for fried rice too. Simmered pork in the refrigerator is indeed my trusty partner for tasty meals.

The only thing I did not like about the recipe was the many hours needed to simmer the meat. However, I found a wonderful solution to the long cooking time.

Last year, my mother gave me her pressure cooker as it was getting too heavy for her to handle. I prepared the recipe using the pressure cooker and found it took only 10 minutes to make perfect simmered pork. To think I spent hundreds of hours in front of a simmering pot all these years. But even without a pressure cooker, you'll find that the time it takes to prepare this dish is well worth it. This is indeed a great recipe.

These days, I enjoy eating this dish with a seasoning paste called *yuzu kosho*, which is made of yuzu citrus and green chillies. The paste is a specialty of Kyushu in southern Japan.

Nibuta Simmered Pork Serves 6–8

900 g (2 lb) boneless pork shoulder

1 leek

1 knob fresh ginger

360 ml (1¹⁄₂ cups) water

180 ml (³⁄₄ cup) sake

180 ml (³⁄₄ cup) Japanese
  soy sauce

180 ml (³⁄₄ cup) mirin

2 Tbsp sugar

mustard or *yuzu kosho*

1. Tie the pork into the shape of a log and secure with kitchen string. Cut off the white part of the leek and save it for another dish as only the green part is used in this recipe for flavouring. Peel and slice the ginger. Place the pork into a pot and add the water, sake, soy sauce, mirin and sugar. (The liquid should cover the meat, so the pot you use shouldn't be too large.) Add the ginger slices and the green part of the leek, left whole. Bring to a boil over medium heat.

2. When the water starts to boil, carefully skim off any fat and foam that rises to the surface of the water. Turn the heat to low and simmer covered for 60–70 minutes, turning the pork occasionally. When the pork is done, turn off the heat and leave the pork to cool in the pot.

3. Discard the leek and ginger slices. Drain the pork and remove the string. Slice the pork into 5-mm (¹⁄₄-inch) thick slices and serve with your choice of vegetables. Skim the excess fat from the sauce and serve with the meat together with mustard or *yuzu kosho.*

When life gives you eggplants...

During this year's extremely hot summer, our refrigerator was always filled with vegetables. Some were from my friends who grow organic vegetables and who would, from time to time, give me some of their harvest. Some were from my children, who have been growing their own favourite vegetables and this year enjoyed a bumper crop of cucumbers, bell peppers (capsicums), cherry tomatoes and eggplants (aubergines). (For my part, I tried to grow some courgettes/zucchini, but failed.)

Among this cornucopia of summer vegetables, the eggplants in the refrigerator presented a constant challenge. There was always a plastic bag of eggplants whose contents never seemed to diminish, despite my best efforts to consume them.

One day, when I was counting the eggplants, somebody knocked on the door.

It was Mrs Kamata, who lives across the street from me. Although she is 91 years old, Mrs Kamata is still healthy and energetic. She told me that she did not need the air conditioner even in the hot summer and that she walked more than half a mile to go marketing almost every morning. She smiled and handed me a plastic bag and told me that her harvest of the day was in it. She advised me to enjoy the contents that day while they were still fresh. Holding the bag in my hands, I somehow knew that it would contain eggplants—and it did!

I appreciated her kindness and the hard work she had put into cultivating the eggplants and I decided to serve them as the main dish that day.

This dish, called *nasu no hasamiage*, is my mom's original recipe and it is the most popular eggplant dish in my family.

Deep-fried Stuffed Eggplants   Serves 4

8 medium eggplants (aubergines)

1/2 onion, peeled and minced

450 g (1 lb) minced pork and beef
  mixture

1 egg, beaten

1/2 tsp salt

1/2 tsp fresh ginger juice

2 Tbsp cornflour (cornstarch)
  or *katakuriko*

50 g (1 3/4 oz) cake flour

16 toothpicks

vegetable oil for deep-frying

Sauce

3 Tbsp Japanese soy sauce

3 Tbsp sake

3 Tbsp mirin

2 Tbsp sugar

1 tsp grated fresh ginger

3 Tbsp chopped spring onion

1. Wash the eggplants and pat dry. Cut off the caps.
   (If you like the unique shape, keep the caps.)

2. In a bowl, combine the minced onion, meat, egg, salt,
   ginger juice and cornflour or *katakuriko*. Mix well.

3. Slice each eggplant into three, starting from the bottom
   and ending about 2 cm (3/4 inch) from the top, so the
   eggplant remains joined at the top. Gently open the slits
   and dust the cut sides with flour. Stuff the meat mixture
   into the slits and dust the surface of the eggplants
   with flour. Secure the eggplants and the mixture with
   toothpicks on both sides.

4. Heat the vegetable oil to 170°C (340°F) in a wok or deep-
   frying pan and deep-fry the stuffed eggplants in batches,
   turning occasionally for 4–5 minutes or until cooked
   through. Drain on a wire rack. Repeat the process until
   all the eggplants are done.

5. Mix all the ingredients for the sauce, except for the
   spring onion, in a frying pan and heat until the sugar
   dissolves. Add the eggplants and cook for a minute,
   turning to coat them with the sauce. Add the spring
   onion and remove from the heat. Remove the toothpicks
   and serve the eggplants with the sauce.

Pasta with a Japanese twist

As three of my four children and my husband were born in the autumn, we hold four birthday parties at this time of the year and often invite our relatives. Given the amount of preparation that is required for those events, I make it a rule to prepare the dessert a day ahead.

I usually make a large salad which I can put together just before everyone arrives, and I choose a main dish which can be cooked in the oven, which makes me feel more relaxed as it leaves me with some spare time.

After all the guests arrive, I start by serving large helpings of pasta to make sure everybody gets enough to eat. I have a very interesting recipe for spaghetti that I learnt from a friend, and I often serve it at these birthday parties. The recipe—spaghetti with turnip and *shiokonbu* (shredded salted kelp)—is based on traditional spaghetti *peperoncini*. I had never thought of adding *shiokonbu* to pasta before learning the recipe. For me, *shiokonbu* was something meant only for using with *onigiri* rice balls or *ochazuke* (rice in hot green tea).

My friend, Taeko, learnt the recipe from a nice little Italian restaurant that was located near the train station where I lived, until they moved a few years ago. Besides basic Italian pasta, they also served original pasta dishes with many interesting ingredients, such as Chinese cabbage, mizuna leaves and edamame beans.

Taeko shared with me that the key to this dish was *umekonbucha* (plum-flavoured seaweed tea powder). Since then, I have always kept *umekonbucha* and a small pack of *shiokonbu* in my kitchen drawer and this dish is now one of my favourite pasta recipes.

Spaghetti with Turnip and Shiokonbu   Serves 4

4 cloves garlic

2–3 dried red chillies

4 turnips with leaves

4 Tbsp olive oil

400 g (14 oz) spaghetti

30 g (1 oz) *shiokonbu*

2 tsp *umekonbucha* powder

1. Peel and slice the garlic. Slice the dried chillies and discard the seeds, which are extremely hot. Slice the seeded dried chillies thinly. Cut the stalks of the turnip leaves into 4–5 cm (1¹/₂–2 inch) lengths, but discard the leaves. Peel the turnips and cut into halves. Slice the halves into 5-mm (¹/₄-inch) thick semicircular pieces.

2. In a frying pan, heat the olive oil, garlic and dried chilli slices over low heat. When the garlic starts to change colour, turn off the heat. Remove the garlic and dried chilli slices and set aside. Add the turnip to the frying pan and cook for 3–4 minutes over medium heat until heated through but still crisp. Add the turnip stalks and cook for 1 minute before removing from the heat.

3. Cook the spaghetti in a large pot of boiling salted water. Drain, reserving 120 ml (¹/₂ cup) of the water. To the pan of turnips, add the *shiokonbu*, *umekonbucha* powder, garlic, dried chilli slices and the reserved hot water. Heat the mixture and combine it with the spaghetti. Serve.

Donabe for two… or six?

I believe that every Japanese family owns a *donabe*, an earthenware pot which can be used for cooking over a stove at the table. In the first winter after we were married, my husband and I went to a department store and bought a *donabe*. There were *donabe* of various sizes, from tiny ones for one person to very large ones.

Obviously, a small *donabe* was sufficient for just the two of us, but my husband insisted that we buy a large one, saying, "*Dai wa sho o kaneru*" (Too big is better than too small.) As I imagined that we would be inviting guests for *nabe* parties, I agreed with him. After buying the *donabe* however, we seldom had guests over when we used the *donabe*.

For two of us, the *donabe* was too big, and we would always end up eating our *donabe* dinners without exchanging a word as we rushed, unsuccessfully, to eat the ingredients before they became overcooked.

We still have the *donabe* and use it often during winter. *Donabe* with meatballs, Chinese cabbage and *harusame* noodles is a dish I often cook when the weather is cold.

However, to tell the truth, I do not cook using the *donabe* anymore. As we now have four growing children with big appetites that often overwhelm my husband and I, our *donabe* is too small. I usually cook the dish in a large stainless steel pot, then serve it in the *donabe*. As soon as everybody gets their first serving, I refill the *donabe* with more food from the large pot!

When I complained to my sister, a ceramic artist, about the size of our *donabe*, she made me a large and deep *donabe*. I am looking forward to using it without worrying about portion sizes.

You may use a *donabe* for this dish, but it's not essential. This dish can be prepared using a regular pot, then served on individual serving plates.

Simmered Meatballs and Chinese Cabbage   Serves 4–6

1 medium onion

600 g (1¹⁄₃ lb) minced pork and beef
   mixture

2 Tbsp + 4 Tbsp cornflour
   (cornstarch) or *katakuriko*

1 egg

salt, as needed

ground black pepper

1 Tbsp vegetable oil

100 g (3¹⁄₂ oz) *harusame* noodles

¹⁄₂ head Chinese cabbage

1 knob fresh ginger

800 ml (3¹⁄₃ cups) water

2 tsp instant dashi powder

50 ml (¹⁄₅ cup) Japanese soy sauce

50 ml (¹⁄₅ cup) mirin

1 Tbsp oyster sauce

4 Tbsp water if using cornflour
   or 2 Tbsp water if using *katakuriko*

1. Peel and finely chop the onion. In a bowl, mix the minced meat, onion, 2 Tbsp cornflour or *katakuriko* and egg. Season with 1 tsp salt and a dash of pepper. Mix well with your hands until the mixture becomes sticky. Form mixture into 16 meatballs. In a frying pan, heat the vegetable oil over medium heat. Brown the meatballs, turning occasionally until they are golden all over. Set aside.

2. Cover the *harusame* noodles with boiling water. Allow to stand for 3–4 minutes, then drain. Cut the Chinese cabbage in half lengthwise, then cut each half into 5-cm (2-inch) wide pieces. Peel and grate the ginger.

3. In a pot, heat the 800 ml (3¹⁄₃ cups) water, dashi powder, soy sauce, mirin, grated ginger, oyster sauce and 1 tsp salt. Add the Chinese cabbage and cook covered over medium heat for 5 minutes. Add the meatballs and simmer for 15–20 minutes, skimming foam and fat occasionally from the surface. Add the drained *harusame* noodles and simmer for 2–3 minutes. Mix the 4 Tbsp cornflour with the 4 Tbsp water and stir in. Mix well and simmer for 2–3 minutes until the sauce has thickened. Dish out and serve.

Tart for the New Year holidays

The New Year holiday season is coming soon. How do you usually spend New Year's Eve?

When I was a child, I looked forward to watching *Kohaku Utagassen* (Red and White Song Contest), the very popular annual NHK TV programme which would start at around 7 pm on December 31 and finish 15 minutes before midnight. As a young child, it was a challenge for me to stay up until the end of the programme, and I remember that it was still quite difficult for me to stay up even when I was a middle school student.

In those days, most grocery stores were closed for the first three days of the New Year and I remember how busy the mothers would be in the days leading up to the New Year, with grocery shopping and preparing *osechi ryori* (traditional New Year's dishes).

Each year, my mother would still be busy in the kitchen even after the show started, preparing *osechi ryori* and ingredients for *zoni* (a soup with chunks of mochi rice cake, chicken, vegetables and other ingredients that are especially popular during the New Year). She would ask me to prepare some desserts for the holiday while she finished the cooking.

Once, there was some leftover sweet potatoes from the *kuri-kinton* (sweet chestnuts dressed with sweet potato paste) in the *osechi ryori*, so I made a sweet potato tart. As the tart is rich and keeps well, we got to enjoy thin slices of the tart throughout the holidays. I was especially happy to sit at the *kotatsu*—a low table with a heater attached to the underside—watching TV and enjoying a piece of tart. Since then, sweet potato tart became a special New Year's dessert for my family.

Now, as a mother myself, I am too busy to prepare dessert on New Year's Eve, but I am pretty sure that my daughter will soon be able to make this tart, just as I did for my family.

Sweet Potato Tart
Makes one 20 cm (8-inch) round tart

Pastry
200 g (7 oz) cake flour

a pinch of salt

120 g (4 oz) butter

60 ml ($^1/_4$ cup) cold water

Filling
450 g (1 lb) sweet potatoes

50 g (1$^3/_4$ oz) butter

100 g (3$^1/_2$ oz) sugar

2 egg yolks

80 ml ($^1/_3$ cup) heavy cream

1 Tbsp rum

Egg Wash
1 egg yolk

1 tsp water

1. To make the pastry, sift the flour into a mixing bowl and add a pinch of salt. Cut the butter into small pieces with a pastry cutter and mix into the flour. Stir in the cold water and blend until the dough holds together. Wrap and chill in the refrigerator until ready to use.

2. For the filling, steam the sweet potatoes until tender. Peel and mash until smooth. Cream the butter in a mixing bowl and add the sweet potato, sugar, 2 of the egg yolks, heavy cream and rum. Mix well and set aside.

3. Preheat the oven to 200°C (400°F). On a lightly floured surface, roll out the chilled pastry into a 5-mm ($^1/_4$-inch) thick sheet. Place the pastry into a lightly buttered 20-cm (8-inch) round tart pan and trim the edges. Prick the bottom of the pastry shell with a fork. Line the pastry with 2 layers of aluminium foil, weighed down with beans or pie weights. Bake for 10 minutes, then remove the foil and beans or weights. Reduce the heat to 180°C (350°F) and bake for 10–15 minutes. Set aside to cool.

4. When the pastry shell is cool to the touch, fill it with the sweet potato mixture and smooth the surface.

5. To make the egg wash, combine the egg yolk and water. Brush the surface of the filling with the egg wash. Bake the tart for 30 minutes or until the surface is golden.

Shiratama Secrets
and Childhood Memories

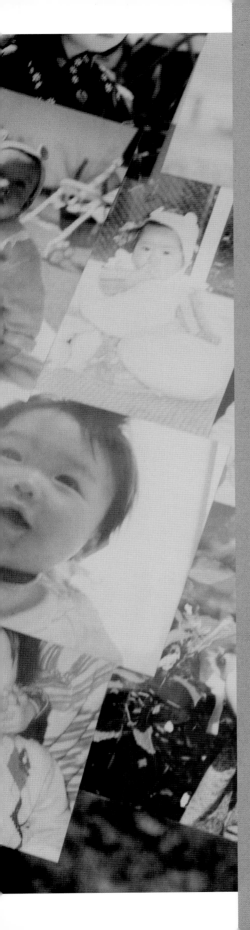

Food to mark a happy start to spring

Have you ever heard of *setsubun*? Although I think February is the coldest month in Japan, the traditional Japanese calendar indicates that with the start of February, spring is just around the corner.

Setsubun, a day in early February, is the traditional end of winter. On this day, a bean-throwing festival is held throughout the country. You can see famous sumo wrestlers on television participating in bean-throwing events held at major temples, tossing beans and small gifts to the crowds.

When I was small, I used to throw soybeans during the festival, shouting, "*Oni wa soto! Fuku wa uchi!* (Out with the devils, in with good fortune!)" As a mother, I remember my children making devil masks at kindergarten and throwing peanuts at their masked teacher. It was funny that they threw peanuts in shells instead of soybeans, but this was so they could eat the nuts later.

Although such *setsubun* events are familiar to those of us who live in the Tokyo region, about seven years ago, I learnt of a different custom practiced in the Osaka/Kyoto region. There, it is quite common to eat *futomaki*, a thick roll of sushi rice wrapped in nori (dried seaweed), on *setsubun*.

My neighbours at that time, the Nishinos, were from Osaka and the mother explained that their custom was to eat a whole *futomaki* with seven kinds of filling while facing *eho*, the direction that was considered lucky for the year. She added that they were not supposed to speak until they had finished eating the whole *futomaki* (or *ehomaki*).

It's amusing to imagine all the members of the Nishino family gazing in the same direction while munching on their *futomaki* without speaking a single word. I was very intrigued with this interesting custom and since then, I always think of the Nishinos (who have returned to Osaka) whenever I eat *futomaki*.

VARIATION You can add two more ingredients to the *futomaki* rolls, such as braised *kanpyo* (dried gourd shavings), boiled prawns (shrimp) or cucumber, to make auspicious *futomaki* with seven kinds of filling.

SUSHI VINEGAR You can use store-bought sushi vinegar or make your own using 6 Tbsp rice vinegar, 4 Tbsp sugar and 2 tsp salt.

Futomaki Rolls

Makes 4 large rolls

6 dried shiitake mushrooms

300 ml (1¼ cups) warm water

480 g (17 oz) uncooked Japanese rice

720 ml (3 cups) water

100 ml (²/₅ cup) sushi vinegar

4 eggs

a pinch of salt

1 tsp vegetable oil

2 Tbsp mirin

2 Tbsp Japanese soy sauce

½ tsp dashi powder

²/₃ *unagi kabayaki* (ready-grilled eel fillet), see Note on page 54

120 g (4 oz) spinach

4 large sheets nori seaweed

12 crab sticks

1. Briefly wash the shiitake, then soak in the warm water for 1–2 hours or overnight for the best flavour. (If possible, keep the stalks pointing downward while soaking.) If you are in a hurry, place the shiitake in the water, microwave for 2 minutes and let the shiitake soak in the water until the water cools.

2. Cook the rice with the water following the instructions on page 126. Transfer the cooked rice into a moistened *handai* (shallow wooden tub for mixing sushi) or a large mixing bowl. Sprinkle the sushi vinegar evenly over the rice. Gently mix the rice with a rice paddle, using mostly vertical motions rather than stirring. Spread the rice evenly in the tub or bowl and let cool to room temperature.

3. Make an egg crêpe to use later as one of the fillings. Beat the 4 eggs in a small bowl with a pinch of salt. Heat the vegetable oil in an 18-cm (7-inch) frying pan over medium heat. Pour the egg into the frying pan and turn the heat to low. Cook covered for 4 minutes or until the surface is almost set. Flip the crêpe over and cook for 1 minute on the other side as though making a pancake.

4. When the caps of the shiitake have become tender, remove from the water (reserving the water) and cut off the hard stem. Add the mirin, soy sauce and dashi powder to the reserved water and bring to a boil. Add the mushrooms and simmer, covered, for 10–15 minutes, then let cool. Gently press out the excess liquid and slice the mushrooms into 8-mm (⅓-inch) thick pieces.

5. Cut the *unagi* lengthwise into 1-cm (½-inch) wide strips. Cut the egg crêpe into 1-cm (½-inch) wide strips. Blanch the spinach in boiling water. Drain, then place in cold water for a few minutes to cool. Drain again. Wring out the excess water and trim off the root ends.

6. Place a sheet of nori smooth side down on a bamboo rolling mat, with the narrower side of the nori toward you. Using wet fingers, spread a quarter of the sushi rice flat onto the nori, leaving a 4-cm (1½-inch) margin at the far end and a 1-cm (½-inch) margin at the near end. About a third of the way in from the near side of the rice, place a quarter each of the eel, egg, spinach, shiitake and crab sticks. Make a roll by rolling the mat away from you and holding it firmly to keep the filling intact as you roll. The filling should be in the centre. Wrap tightly with plastic wrap until ready to serve. Just before serving, remove the plastic wrap and cut into 2-cm (¾-inch) thick slices.

Yuzu cookies, a tangy winter treat

We have a large *natsumikan* (bitter summer orange) tree in our garden, which yields more than a hundred large, yellow *natsumikan* every year. This is thanks to my great-grandmother, who ate a very tasty *natsumikan* more than 40 years ago and planted one of the seeds. However, we are accustomed to the improved variety of the fruit sold nowadays in stores and we use the sour-tasting *natsumikan* from the tree only when making marmalade.

The family living next to us has a small tangerine tree in their garden, which produces masses of bright orange fruit at the end of each year. On those weekends, my children would visit the garden with their scissors to pick tangerines. The fresh fruit from the tree is very tasty and my kids are always happy with their harvest.

There is also a lovely yuzu citrus tree in the neighbour's garden and swallowtail butterflies often lay eggs on its leaves in the summer. My younger sons would be extremely excited when they find the eggs and used to bring them back home to raise into butterflies. After the caterpillars hatched from the eggs, the boys would feed them fresh leaves every day until they formed chrysalis. Once, after one of the butterflies emerged, one of my sons took it to our neighbour's tree and released it at the same place where he had found the eggs.

During the winter, our neighbour's tree is always weighed down with hundreds of yuzu and we are allowed to visit the garden whenever we want fresh yuzu. Whenever there is an excess of yuzu, my daughter and I like to make yuzu cookies with yuzu icing.

My children are now collecting yuzu seeds to grow their own wonderful yuzu tree in our garden. However, I am not sure if my sons will still be fascinated with swallowtail butterflies once the tree has grown.

SUBSTITUTE FOR YUZU If yuzu is not in season, it can be substituted with lemon.

Yuzu Cookies   Makes about 40 cookies

Cookies

1 yuzu

100 g (3¹/₂ oz) butter

4 Tbsp sugar

1 egg yolk

200 g (7 oz) cake flour, sifted

Icing

6 Tbsp icing (confectioner's) sugar

1 Tbsp yuzu juice

1. Wash the yuzu and carefully grate only the yellow rind of the fruit. (Don't use the inner white part as it is bitter.) In a bowl, cream the butter. Add the sugar and whisk until fluffy. Add the egg yolk and whisk. Add the flour and the grated yuzu rind and gently fold. Shape the dough into a flattened ball. Cover with plastic wrap and place in the refrigerator for 30 minutes.

2. Preheat the oven to 170°C (340°F). Roll out the dough so it is 6–7 mm (¹/₄–¹/₃-inch) thick and cut into 3-cm (1¹/₄-inch) square pieces. Place on a baking sheet and bake in the oven for about 10 minutes or until lightly coloured. Remove from the oven and let cool.

3. To make the icing, combine the icing sugar and yuzu juice in a small cup and whisk well. Using a teaspoon, glaze the top of the cookies with yuzu icing while the cookies are still slightly warm. Let stand until the icing hardens. Store in an airtight container.

73

Little orphaned potato finds a good home (and makes a good meal)

Soon after the harvest in October, my nine-year-old son found a tiny potato when passing through a nearby vegetable field. We figured the potato had been left there because it was too small and a bit green. My son brought it home and put it in his drawer together with other his treasures such as pine cones, acorns and stones.

After a while, he was surprised to find the potato sprouting in his drawer. He then decided to grow it in a container of soil and started avidly taking care of the small potato and looking forward to the harvest. He would watch the potato and count the leaves before going to school every day. He watered and talked to the potato, naming it *Jagaimo-chan* (Little Potato).

When the potato leaves began to turn yellow in January, I urged him to dig it out. But he said, "No, I feel sorry for the potato." He loved his potato so much. At the beginning of February, however, he finally decided to harvest his potatoes.

Harvesting the potatoes was a very straightforward process. My son simply turned the container upside down to extract the tiny potatoes. He happily picked the potatoes out of the soil and proudly showed them to his brothers and sister. He washed the potatoes and made tasty miso soup with them all by himself out of respect for the harvest.

Marvelling at the fate of the abandoned potato, I said to my son, "Don't you think this is nothing but a miracle of God?"

He replied, "Yes, of course. But what about my efforts?"

Here is a recipe for braised potatoes and minced chicken, a popular dish calling for the new potatoes that will hit the shelves at this time of the year.

QUICK DASHI STOCK If you do not have home-made dashi stock on hand, make up some using 400 ml (1 2/3 cups) water and 1 tsp instant dashi stock.

Braised New Potatoes with Minced Chicken   Serves 4–6

800 g (1³/₄ lb) new potatoes

1 small onion

1 knob fresh ginger

vegetable oil, as needed

200 g (7 oz) minced chicken

400 ml (1²/₃ cups) dashi stock (page 127)

3 Tbsp Japanese soy sauce

3 Tbsp mirin

2 Tbsp cornflour (cornstarch) or 1 Tbsp *katakuriko*

2 Tbsp water or 1 Tbsp water if using *katakuriko*

1. Wash and dry the potatoes. Peel and chop the onion. Peel and grate the ginger. In a deep-frying pan, heat enough vegetable oil for deep-frying to 170°C (340°F). Deep-fry the potatoes in small batches for 2–3 minutes per batch, turning occasionally until the skin becomes crisp. Drain on a wire rack. At this point, the potatoes need not be completely cooked through. (If you are in a hurry, you can stir-fry the potatoes instead of deep-frying them.)

2. In another frying pan, heat 1 Tbsp vegetable oil and cook the onion over medium heat until it becomes semi-transparent. Add the minced chicken and cook, stirring constantly until heated through.

3. Put the dashi stock, soy sauce, mirin and grated ginger into a pot. Add the deep-fried potatoes and the chicken-and-onion mixture. Simmer covered for 20 minutes or until potatoes are tender.

4. In a small cup, combine the cornflour or *katakuriko* and the water. Stir the mixture into the pot until the sauce thickens. Remove from the heat and serve.

The secret to colourful shiratama dessert

Since finishing the entrance exams for middle school in early February, my 12-year-old daughter has been enjoying cooking. Although she loves to make things in the kitchen, she was too busy to do so while going to cram school. She was not even able to enjoy eating with us most nights, as she took a bento dinner to school four times a week. But now she is relaxed and spends her time in the kitchen, cooking her favourite desserts almost every day.

Shiratama dango—dumplings made from rice flour—is one of her favourite recipes, and she has created many interesting varieties. One day, she served us orange-coloured *shiratama*, although *shiratama* are usually white. (In fact, the word *shiratama* literally means white ball.) Curious, I asked her how she made them orange. However, she answered flatly, "I can't tell you. It's a trade secret."

The next time she prepared the dessert, the *shiratama* were pink. Another time, they were green. She finally relented and told me how to make the coloured *shiratama*.

For the orange *shiratama*, she added puréed *mikan* oranges to the *shiratamako* flour instead of water. She used strawberries for the pink *shiratama* and kiwi fruit for the green ones. She served those pretty coloured *shiratama* with ice cream or with milk or coconut milk sweetened with sugar. She also made a simple *shiratama* fruit salad, neatly served with strawberries and canned fruit. Her younger brothers were thrilled to try her new creations on a nearly daily basis.

Her fruit salad topped with *shiratama* made me feel nostalgic for the *shiratama* fruit salad my grandmother used to make. But my grandmother's recipe was for *shiratama* made in the traditional way, by combining *shiratamako* flour and water. My daughter substituted tofu for the water to make tofu *shiratama*, a recipe given to us by a friend of mine. It may seem strange to combine *shiratamako* flour with tofu, but tofu makes the dumplings tender and incredibly tasty. The tofu *shiratama* tastes good simply with maple syrup or *kuromitsu*—a traditional Japanese syrup made from brown sugar.

Tofu Shiratama with Fruit   Serves 6

3 slices canned pineapple

3 pieces canned peach

1 small can oranges

1 kiwi fruit

360 ml (1¹/₂ cups) syrup (reserved from canned fruit)

1 Tbsp sugar

6 strawberries

200 g (7 oz) *shiratamako* flour

300 g (10¹/₂ oz) block soft tofu, lightly drained

1. Drain the pineapple, peach and oranges, and reserve the syrup. Cut each pineapple slice into 8 pieces. Cut the peach into small pieces. Peel the kiwi and slice into small pieces. Combine the syrup from the canned fruit to make 360 ml (1¹/₂ cups). Add the sugar and stir well. Wash, hull and drain the strawberries. Cut into quarters.

2. In a bowl, combine the *shiratamako* flour and tofu. Mix well with your hands. To make *shiratama dango* dumplings, roll one teaspoonful of the dough with both hands into a ball. Hold the ball between your thumb and index finger and slightly press it in the middle. (It is often said that *shiratamako* dough has to be "as hard as a earlobe". If makig regular *shiratamako*, use 190–200 ml (6¹/₃–6³/₄ fl oz) water instead of tofu. Add the water little by little until the right consistency is achieved.

3. Bring a pot of water to a boil and add the *shiratama* one by one. When the *shiratama* rises to the surface of the water, scoop it out with a perforated ladle. Drain and place in a bowl of iced water. When all the *shiratama* are done, drain them.

4. Divide the pineapple, peach, orange and kiwi pieces among 6 individual serving bowls. Arrange the *shiratama* and strawberries on top and pour the syrup over the arranged items. Serve.

Garlic soy sauce infusion from Okinawa

During the spring vacation, I visited Okinawa Prefecture for four days with my family. I like going there at this time of the year because the weather is wonderful and the airfare is also quite reasonable compared with the rates in the summer.

Whenever we are there, we enjoy eating traditional Okinawan dishes at small restaurants for most of our meals. However, for dinner on the last night of our recent trip, we decided to go to a famous steak restaurant in the hotel where we were staying.

Of course, the sizzling steak was wonderful, but I was also very impressed with the tasty sauce that accompanied the steak. Although I thought it might be impolite, I still went ahead to ask the waiter if he could get me the recipe for the sauce. The waiter seemed a little put off initially, but he headed to the kitchen to talk to the chef. When he returned, he proudly informed us that it was a "secret sauce"—and then revealed the recipe. I found it unbelievable at first, as the waiter had said that all that was needed to make the sauce was to soak peeled garlic in a jar of soy sauce for a month.

As soon as I got home, I made a large jar of the garlic soy sauce. The sauce has now aged sufficiently and I have enjoyed it in many dishes such as stir-fried vegetables and fried chicken. I have also used it to flavour the stock in which I simmer ingredients for other dishes.

Here is a recipe for barbecue pork I made with the garlic soy sauce for a barbecue party the other day. Although it started raining, we still had a good time and the broiled pork was popular among my friends and family as the meat was very tender and juicy, thanks to the grated apple and onion that are also part of the recipe.

Although you can leave the pork in the refrigerator to marinate in the sauce for two to three days before cooking, I recommend preparing a double portion of the recipe and freezing half of it after a few hours of marination. This way, you can have home-made barbecue pork whenever you feel like it, just by defrosting and grilling it. I am sure a slice or two would go nicely in a bento box as well.

GARLIC SOY SAUCE To make the garlic soy sauce, peel 7–8 cloves of garlic and place them with 1 litre (4 cups) of Japanese soy sauce in a clean jar. Let it sit for a month. For a quick fix, mix 4 Tbsp Japanese soy sauce with 1 clove of grated garlic.

Barbecue Pork with Garlic Soy Sauce Serves 4

¹/₄ onion

¹/₄ apple

1 knob fresh ginger

4 Tbsp garlic soy sauce

4 Tbsp mirin

4 slices pork loin, each 1-cm
(¹/₂-inch) thick and about 150 g
(5¹/₄ oz) per slice

1. Peel the onion, apple and ginger and grate into a bowl. Add the garlic soy sauce and mirin. Soak the pork slices overnight in the refrigerator or for at least 3 hours.

2. Preheat the oven to 220°C (425°F). Broil the pork slices for 10 minutes on a broiler pan. Turn the meat over and cook for 5 more minutes or until golden and cooked through. Serve with your choice of vegetables.

Special treatment for cabbage in Osaka-style okonomiyaki

Have you ever tried *okonomiyaki*—the Japanese savoury pancake that is cooked on a hot plate and filled with a variety of ingredients? For many years, I didn't care for this dish, as I had few chances to taste it and I never came across a decent recipe.

However, about seven years ago, our neighbours, the Nishinos from Osaka, made us some wonderful *okonomiyaki* using their own recipe. Every part of the cooking process was fascinating.

Firstly, they do not wash the cabbage used in *okonomiyaki*. When I asked why, Mrs Nishino explained that the moisture left on the leaves after washing the cabbage would spoil the consistency of the pancake mix. Secondly, while I usually made *okonomiyaki* with coarse pieces of chopped cabbage, they used a whole cabbage and finely chopped it. I was surprised again when I learnt that they would never prepare *okonomiyaki* without some *nagaimo* (yam). I did not think that such a small amount of this long, white root vegetable would have such an important role in *okonomiyaki*. Fourthly, they handled all the ingredients

very carefully and instead of combining everything at once, they used several small bowls and mixed the ingredients together just before pouring the mixture onto the hot plate. Thanks to the amount of finely chopped cabbage, Mrs Nishino's *okonomiyaki* was fluffy and tasted very delicate.

While I was making croquettes with Mrs Nishino some time later, I was careful to ask if I could wash the cabbage before shredding it. She seemed rather upset at my request as she exclaimed, "Of course!" Given her reaction, I am sure that *okonomiyaki* is the only dish in which the Nishinos use unwashed cabbage.

HOME-MADE OKONOMIYAKI SAUCE If you can't get hold of ready-made *okonomiyaki* sauce, make your own with 4 Tbsp of ready-made *tonkatsu* sauce, 4 Tbsp of tomato ketchup and 2 Tbsp of Japanese soy sauce.

VARIATION 1 If you can get hold of *agedama*, the crunchy pieces of fried flour dough that can be found in Japanese supermarkets, it will add flavour to your *okonomiyaki*. Add 2 Tbsp of *agedama* to the batter, cabbage, egg and *benishoga* mixture in step 2 of the recipe.

VARIATION 2 Add other ingredients such as squid or scallops to your *okonomiyaki*.

Okonomiyaki   Serves 4

50 g (1³/₄ oz) *nagaimo* (yam)

130 g (4¹/₂ oz) cake flour or *okonomiyaki* flour

240 ml (1 cup) water or dashi stock

a pinch of salt

¹/₄ head cabbage

200 g (7 oz) thinly sliced pork rib meat

4 eggs

4 tsp *benishoga* pickled ginger

200 g (7 oz) prawns (shrimp)

okonomiyaki sauce to serve

mayonnaise to serve, optional

dried bonito flakes to serve, optional

aonori powdered seaweed to serve, optional

1. Peel and grate the *nagaimo*. In a bowl, mix the flour, water or dashi stock, salt and *nagaimo* and mix well. Discard the hard core of the cabbage and finely chop. Cut the pork into thin bite-size pieces and cook on a hot plate at 230°C (450°F) until it is heated through. Set the pork aside. Reserve the hot plate with the residual pork fat for cooking the *okonomiyaki*.

2. In a separate small bowl, combine a ladleful of batter, a quarter of the chopped cabbage, 1 egg and 1 tsp *benishoga*.

3. Reheat the hot plate used for cooking the pork. Pour the batter onto the hot plate, forming a circle about 15 cm (6 inch) in diameter. Cook for 3–4 minutes. While the *okonomiyaki* mix is cooking, grill the prawns on another part of the hot plate.

4. When the surface of the *okonomiyaki* begins to set, top it with a quarter of the pork and prawns. Cook for 1–2 minutes, then turn the *okonomiyaki* over with a spatula. Cook for 3–4 minutes, then turn it over again.

5. Repeat the process to make three more *okonomiyaki* pancakes. Spread *okonomiyaki* sauce and mayonnaise on top of each *okonomiyaki* and sprinkle with bonito flakes and *aonori*. Serve.

Childhood memories linger in a field of beans

While taking our dog for a walk the other day, I noticed that *sora-mame* beans—called broad beans or fava beans in English—were ready to be harvested in one corner of a large vegetable field.

Have you ever seen *sora-mame* on a stalk? As the word *sora-mame* literally translates as sky bean, I used to think the name meant sky-coloured beans. When I saw them on a stalk for the first time, however, I realized the true meaning behind the name. The thick, dark green pods rose skyward directly from the stalk, giving them a unique look and hence their name.

Even before I was born, there was a huge vegetable field in my neighbourhood. I often enjoyed walking through the field—which spanned about 36 hectares. The local children were allowed to cultivate vegetables in a part of the field and they also looked forward to the annual school race that was held on a path running through the field.

However, at the end of last year, a development project began on that piece of land, and the children had to give up their vegetable patch. The field was always covered with greenery at this time of the year, but this year, many of the full-time farmers who had been using the field are not cultivating vegetables there anymore.

Before the construction started, the schoolchildren were surveyed about what kind of facilities they hoped to have on the developed land. There were several choices, such as houses, a park or shops, but my daughter told me many children wanted nothing but the vegetable field left as it was. Seeing the thick green *sora-mame* growing in the corner of the field reminded me of the children having to give up their vegetable patch and I felt a little sad.

Somebody knocked on my door as I was writing this. It was my 92-year-old neighbour, Mrs Kamata, and she was holding a large plastic bag full of *sora-mame* beans freshly harvested from her vegetable garden. I'm looking forward to preparing some *sora-mame* dishes while the beans are in season.

VARIATION This dish is also good served warm without being puréed.

Cold Sora-mame Potage Serves 4

salt, as needed

200 g (7 oz) shelled broad beans or about 800 g (1³/₄ lb) broad beans with pods, shelled

1 potato

1 small onion

10 g (¹/₃ oz) butter

400 ml (1²/₃ cups) water

1 bouillon cube

400 ml (1²/₃ cups) milk

8 boiled and shelled prawns (shrimp)

1 Tbsp heavy cream

1. Add 1 tsp salt to a saucepan of water and bring to a boil. Add the broad beans and boil for 2 minutes. Drain. Let the beans cool and remove the skins. Reserve 8 well-shaped beans for the garnish.

2. Peel and cut the potato into 5-mm (¹/₄-inch) thick fan-shaped slices. Peel and chop the onion.

3. In a small pan, heat the butter and sauté the onion until semi-transparent. Add the potato, water and bouillon cube. Cook, covered, over low to medium heat for 10–15 minutes until the potato is tender.

4. Add the peeled broad beans, milk and ¹/₂ tsp salt. Simmer for 2–3 minutes, then remove from the heat and let cool. Pour the mixture into a food processor and purée.

5. Pour the purée into a sealed container or a saucepan with a lid and chill in the refrigerator until ready to serve. Serve in individual bowls, garnishing the top of each serving with the prawns, reserved beans and heavy cream.

Eel sushi to wriggle your way out of summer weariness

On a certain day in late July, eels are sold as the main item in supermarkets and the food halls of department stores. You may find *nobori* (long, narrow, vertical flags), displaying the word *unagi* to promote sales on that day.

The day, known as *Doyo no Ushi no Hi*, falls between mid July and early August. *Doyo* does not mean Saturday (*doyobi*), but refers to a period of 18 days at the end of the season. Each *doyo* has one or two *Ushi no Hi* or days of the ox, named for one of the 12 animals of the Chinese zodiac. On the first day of the ox of the summer *doyo*, people are encouraged to eat grilled eel to beat summer weariness.

When my daughter turned one, we went to a *unagi* restaurant to have special *unaju* (rice topped with glaze-grilled eel called *unagi no kabayaki*, served in a lacquered box). I thought *unagi* would be too greasy to give to a baby, so I had already fed my daughter her baby food in advance. However, when the *unagi* was served, she started sniffing about, looking for the sweet smelling item on the table. As she looked so earnest, I gave her just a little bit of *unagi* flavoured rice. She immediately started laughing, swinging her hips from side to side in a kind of dance, leaning on the table as she could not stand on her own yet. Her reaction was so adorable that I continued giving her the *unagi* flavoured rice. Every time she had a bite, she did a little dance with a big smile. She still loves *unagi* and whenever we visit the restaurant, we talk about her *unagi* 'debut'.

As eels are usually expensive on *Doyo no Ushi no Hi*, I don't buy them on that day, but on the following day, when they are put on sale. Then I keep them in my freezer.

Eel and cucumber *chirashi-zushi* (mixed sushi) is a quick and tasty dish I often cook during the summer, especially on days when I do not feel like going shopping, as all the ingredients are readily at hand in my kitchen.

SUSHI VINEGAR You can use store-bought sushi vinegar or make your own using 3 Tbsp of rice vinegar, 2 Tbsp of sugar and 1 tsp of salt.

Eel and Cucumber Chirashi-zushi   Serves 4

480 g (17 oz) uncooked Japanese rice

720 ml (3 cups) water

4 Tbsp sushi vinegar

1 *myoga* bud

6 shiso leaves

2 cucumbers

1/3 tsp salt

2 *unagi kabayaki* (ready-grilled eel fillet), see Note on page 54

kabayaki no tare eel sauce (a sweet soy sauce-based sauce usually included with package of grilled eel)

1 Tbsp toasted white sesame seeds

1. Cook the rice with the water following the instructions on page 126. Transfer the cooked rice into a moistened *handai* (shallow wooden tub for mixing sushi) or a large mixing bowl. Sprinkle the sushi vinegar evenly over the rice. Gently mix the rice with a rice paddle, using mostly vertical motions rather than stirring. Spread the rice evenly in the tub or bowl and let cool to room temperature.

2. Wash and shred the *myoga* bud. Wash the shiso leaves and pat dry with a paper towel. Cut the shiso leaves into halves lengthwise and shred thinly. Slice the cucumbers into thin rounds. Sprinkle with salt, leave for 5 minutes, then lightly squeeze in a paper towel to remove excess moisture. Cut the eel into halves lengthwise, then into 6-mm (1/4-inch) wide pieces. Drizzle with *kabayaki no tare*.

3. Sprinkle *myoga*, shiso and toasted sesame seeds onto the rice and gently mix them in, again using mostly vertical motions rather than stirring. Add the cucumber slices and mix again. Serve the rice on individual plates and top with the eel.

Refreshing Japan-made Chinese noodles

Summer vacation has started and it is really annoying for me to have to cook three times a day for four children who have wonderful appetites.

During the school summer holidays, I repeatedly serve my children cold noodle dishes such as *somen* or *hiyashi chuka* for lunch. These dishes, which are served with a variety of toppings and a sour sauce, are easy to prepare.

Even though *chuka*, meaning Chinese, is part of its name, *hiyashi chuka* is a dish that originated in Japan. It is one of the most popular summertime dishes. It used to be served only during summer at Chinese restaurants or ramen noodle shops, but as there were so many fans of *hiyashi chuka* (who might even be called *hiyashi chuka otaku*) who look forward to the moment when *hiyashi chuka* returns to the menu each summer, some restaurants have started serving the dish throughout the year.

When I prepare *hiyashi chuka* for lunch, I top the noodles with just a few standard toppings such as ham, cucumbers, shredded egg crêpe and tomatoes.

When I cook it for dinner, however, I try to use other kinds of toppings, such as boiled chicken, scallops or prawns (shrimp), to make the dish somewhat special. My children call it *gochiso* (gourmet) *hiyashi chuka* to distinguish it from my regular *hiyashi chuka*.

I am sure that *gochiso hiyashi chuka* will be appreciated if you serve it to your family or friends on a hot summer day.

VARIATION 1 You can use fresh Chinese noodles to make this dish. Make your own sauce by combining 300 ml (1¼ cups) of chicken stock, 6 Tbsp of Japanese soy sauce, 6 Tbsp of rice vinegar, 2 Tbsp of sugar and 1 tsp of sesame oil.

VARIATION 2 If you can get hold of sashimi scallops, I suggest substituting them for the regular scallops in this recipe, as they have a wonderful texture and taste. To prepare, bring water to a boil in a saucepan and add a pinch of salt. Add the scallops and cook for 1 minute until they start to turn white on the outside. Drain and cool in iced water. Drain again and pat dry with a paper towel. Slice the scallops in half horizontally, making 2 discs from each one.

Gochiso Hiyashi Chuka   Serves 4

2 eggs

a pinch of salt

6 slices ham

1 chicken breast, boiled

90 g (3 oz) crab sticks

1 cucumber

1 tomato

8 scallops

4 packs *hiyashi chuka* noodles with
  ready-made sauce

1/2 head lettuce

200 g (7 oz) boiled and shelled
  prawns (shrimp)

mustard, to taste

1. To make the egg crêpes, break the eggs into a bowl and add a pinch of salt. Beat well. Heat a frying pan over medium-low heat and wipe with an oil-soaked pad. Pour a third of the egg mixture into the pan and tilt the pan so that the egg spreads evenly. When surface is set, flip the egg and cook for a few seconds on the other side. Wipe the pan with the oil-soaked pad and repeat the process. When done, cut the egg crêpes into thin strips, about 5 cm (2 inches) long.

2. Cut the ham into thin strips. Shred the chicken and the crab sticks by hand. Julienne the cucumber. Cut the tomato into 8 wedges.

3. Bring water to a boil in a saucepan and add a pinch of salt. Add the scallops and cook for 2–3 minutes or until cooked through. Drain and cool in iced water. Drain again and pat dry with a paper towel. Slice the scallops in half horizontally, making 2 discs from each one.

4. Cook the noodles in a large pot of boiling water, stirring occasionally, for about 3 minutes or for the length of time indicated on the package. When cooked, rinse with cold water and drain.

5. Place the lettuce leaves on 4 individual serving plates and top each with a quarter of the noodles. Arrange the egg crêpes, ham, chicken, crab stick, cucumber, tomato, scallops and prawns neatly on top of the noodles, being careful not to mix the toppings together.

6. Pour the ready-made sauce for *hiyashi chuka* on top of the noodles. Serve with a dab of mustard on the side.

Spinach and fried eggs brighten a simple curry

Curry is a very popular dish among Japanese children and it is easy to prepare. In fact, it is so simple that kids can be taught to make it for themselves. Both of the school camps that two of my children took part in this summer had a curry cooking class.

Like many Japanese, I like to cook curry not only from scratch, but also with instant curry roux, as there are many tasty varieties available. Look for instant curry roux in your local Asian supermarket.

When I have ample time to cook curry, I go for beef or pork, chunks of vegetables such as carrots and potatoes, stir-fried onion and grated apple. When I don't have enough time to let a curry simmer, I choose chicken or seafood with tomatoes, mushrooms and thinly sliced onions as they do not take long to cook. And when I am really in a hurry, I choose minced meat, chopped onion and eggplant (aubergine) as they make the perfect combination to cook in a limited time.

As I cook curry in a large pot, I usually serve the leftovers for lunch the next day. Some of my children complain that the curry is overcooked, as most of the solid ingredients have become dissolved in the curry paste by then.

However, I came up with a special idea that I got at a curry restaurant near an office where I used to work. There was a very popular dish at the restaurant called Popeye curry. This spicy curry, topped with sautéed spinach and crispy deep-fried fish, always caught my attention whenever I visited the restaurant for lunch.

Now, I top my own curry—leftover or freshly made—with sautéed spinach and a soft sunny-side up egg instead of the fried fish. Thanks to this dish, my children eat an incredible amount of spinach.

So if you want to add spinach to your diet or feed spinach to your children, give this recipe a try.

CURRY ROUX Ready-made curry roux is a staple of the Japanese pantry; you should be able to find various brands at your Asian grocery store. If you can't get hold of any, substitute your favourite curry sauce for the roux and the tomato ketchup.

Sunny-side Up Curry   Serves 4

4 eggplants (aubergines)

2 onions

vegetable oil, as needed

400 g (14 oz) minced pork and beef
　mixture

1 litre (4 cups) water

200 g (7 oz) instant curry roux

2 Tbsp tomato ketchup

200 g (7 oz) spinach

10 g ($^1/_3$ oz) butter

salt and ground black pepper

4 eggs

4 plates cooked Japanese rice

1. Slice off the eggplant caps and cut the eggplants into
   1.5-cm ($^3/_4$-inch) thick slices. Soak in a bowl of water.

2. Peel and chop the onions. In a frying pan, heat 1 tsp
   vegetable oil and cook the onions over medium heat
   until semi-transparent. Add the minced meat and stir-
   fry until heated through. In a pot, bring 1 litre (4 cups)
   water to a boil and add the minced meat. Simmer,
   occasionally skimming foam and fat.

3. In a large, clean frying pan, heat 1 Tbsp vegetable oil.
   Drain the eggplants, place in the frying pan and cook for
   3–4 minutes. Add the eggplants to the pot of simmering
   minced meat and continue to simmer, covered, for
   10 minutes. Add the curry roux and tomato ketchup and
   simmer for 5 more minutes, stirring constantly. Remove
   from the heat.

4. Bring a pot of water to a boil and blanch the spinach for
   1 minute. Drain and cool in iced water. Gently squeeze
   the water from the spinach with your hands and trim off
   the ends. Cut into 2.5-cm (1-inch) lengths. In a frying
   pan, heat the butter and briefly cook the spinach. Lightly
   season with salt and pepper. Remove from the heat.

5. Prepare 4 medium-cooked sunny-side up fried eggs.
   Pour the curry over the plates of rice. Top the curry with
   sautéed spinach and sunny-side up eggs. Serve.

Fresh veggies from son's garden to deep-fryer

As my second son loves growing vegetables, this summer, we have been able to eat cucumbers, cherry tomatoes, eggplants (aubergines), potatoes and other vegetables, as well as many kinds of herbs, fresh from his garden.

Among those vegetables, I was especially impressed with the eggplants, which grew so well and tasted great. In Japanese, there is a saying, *"Oya no iken to nasu no hana wa senni hitotsumo mudaganai,"* which means, "There never is waste as far as parents' opinions and eggplant flowers are concerned." Yes, the eggplant flowers almost always grow into tasty eggplants as far as I can tell.

One evening during the summer vacation, I was making marinated pork and deep-fried summer vegetables for dinner. While cooking, I thought it would be nice to make extra portions of the dish to give to my friends. I was able to increase the quantity by simply stepping outside into my son's vegetable garden, picking some eggplants and adding them to the dish. At that moment, I realized how lucky I was to have a son who raises organic vegetables.

By the way, there is also a saying, *"Aki nasu wa yome ni kuwasuna,"* which means, "Don't give eggplant harvested in autumn to your daughter-in-law." Some rationalize that this is because eggplant harvested in autumn cools the body and is not good for the health of young women. Others interpret it to mean that the eggplant is too tasty to waste on your daughter-in-law. I agree that the vegetable is very tasty, but I hope I am never so mean to any of my future daughters-in-law.

This fresh-tasting, marinated dish is one of my favourites. I believe the combination of crispy deep-fried pork, eggplant, bell peppers (capsicums) and pumpkin is simply perfect. If you add some mushrooms, such as *maitake*, it gives the dish an autumnal accent.

VARIATION For extra flavour, add 1 Tbsp of vinegar (I recommend black vinegar) to the sauce before putting in the vegetables.

Marinated Pork and Deep-fried Vegetables   Serves 4–6

4 eggplants (aubergines)

6 green bell peppers (capsicums)

300 g (10½ oz) *kabocha* pumpkin

300 g (10½ oz) thinly sliced pork loin

salt and ground black pepper

240 ml (1 cup) dashi stock (page 127)

4 Tbsp Japanese soy sauce

4 Tbsp mirin

vegetable oil for deep-frying

50 g (1¾ oz) cornflour (cornstarch) or *katakuriko*

1. Trim off the caps of the eggplants and cut into halves lengthwise. Trim the bell peppers and cut into halves lengthwise, removing the seeds. Remove the seeds and spongy parts of the pumpkin and cut it into 5-mm (¼-inch) thick wedges. Pat the vegetables dry with paper towels. Lightly season the pork with salt and pepper.

2. To prepare the sauce, combine the dashi stock, soy sauce and mirin in a saucepan, and bring to a boil. Remove from the heat.

3. In a wok or deep frying pan heat the vegetable oil to 170°C (340°F) and deep-fry the eggplants, turning occasionally, for 2–3 minutes or until cooked through. Drain on a wire rack. Deep-fry the pumpkin slices for 3–4 minutes or until cooked through. Drain on a wire rack. Deep-fry the bell peppers for a minute and drain.

4. Dust the pork slices with the cornflour or *katakuriko* and deep-fry for 2–3 minutes or until they turn golden and crispy. Drain.

5. Pour the sauce into a large, flat-bottom container and put in all the deep-fried ingredients while still warm. Serve warm or let the vegetables and sauce cool and chill in the refrigerator before serving.

Hot daikon dish for cold winter nights with bittersweet roots

Although daikon is sold throughout the year, this long white radish tastes especially great in the winter. There is a vegetable stall behind my house where daikon is sold and once, when my daughter went there to buy daikon, the radishes were sold out. The farmer was kind enough to take her out into the vegetable field just behind the stall and let her pull a large daikon out of the ground by herself. This made my daughter very happy, and I was impressed at how sweet and juicy the fresh daikon was.

Simmered daikon with chicken wings is one of the dishes I love to cook in the winter. This daikon dish reminds me of an English woman I used to be good friends with. She used to live nearby and had been married to a Japanese man for about 10 years. Although she did not like Japanese food much, she used to cook the dishes to please her husband. This recipe for simmered daikon and chicken wings was one of the recipes I gave her. She told me she cooked the dish often as her husband loved it, despite the fact that she did not care for the dish herself.

She also used to make perfectly shaped *onigiri* rice balls with her long fingers. It was amazing how the *onigiri* she made looked like those sold at the stores—their triangular shape was flawless and all her *onigiri* turned out exactly the same size.

She often visited me with her children. When I couldn't go out for a while after giving birth, she would cycle over, balancing her children in their bicycle seats, to bring me food. When I had back pain, she came over with medicine for my back.

Four years ago, just before Christmas, she dropped by and gave my family wonderful presents, as she had always done. Things seemed normal, but I sensed that something wasn't right—each of those presents was too special, and she somehow looked sad. A few days later, she went to England with her three children to spend the Christmas holidays with her mother. As I had imagined, she left her husband and did not return to Japan.

I still cannot forget her beaming smile, beautiful children and perfect triangle-shaped *onigiri*. Whenever I cook simmered daikon with chicken wings, I wonder what went through her mind all those times whenever she prepared her husband's favourite Japanese dish.

Simmered Daikon with Chicken Wings   Serves 4

10 g (¹/₃ oz) died konbu, about
   5 x 15 cm (2 x 6 inch)

1 litre (4 cups) water

1 daikon radish

12 chicken wings

1 knob fresh ginger

120 ml (¹/₂ cup) sake

60 ml (¹/₄ cup) Japanese soy sauce

60 ml (¹/₄ cup) mirin

2 Tbsp sugar

2 tsp salt

1. Wipe the konbu with a damp cloth. Pour the 1 litre (4 cups) of water into a pot, and soak the konbu in it for 30 minutes.

2. Peel the daikon and cut into rounds 3-cm (1¹/₄-inch) thick. If the daikon is especially stout, cut into half-moon shapes. Place the daikon pieces in a separate pot and cover with water. Bring to a boil and simmer for 20–30 minutes or until the daikon is tender. Drain. Rinse with running water and drain again.

3. Remove the konbu from the pot and cut into pieces about 4-cm (1¹/₂-inch) square. Peel and slice the ginger. Add the chicken and ginger slices to the pot from which you have just removed the konbu. Bring to a boil and simmer for 10 minutes, skimming foam from the surface from time to time.

4. Add the daikon, konbu, sake, soy sauce, mirin, sugar and salt to the pot. Simmer, covered, for 50–60 minutes over medium-low heat. Serve.

A love of parent-and-child bowl that skipped a generation

My children love the *oyakodon* that I make. And it makes me very happy when they ask for *oyakodon* for dinner, as the dish is simple to prepare. I need only chicken, onion and eggs—along with rice, which is always on hand—and it takes less than 15 minutes to cook. The name *oyakodon* literally means parent-and-child bowl. As the dish is made with chicken and eggs, it's a fitting name.

I used to work at an office near Nihonbashi, Tokyo, and there was a very famous *oyakodon* restaurant nearby. *Oyakodon* is said to have originated from this restaurant more than a hundred years ago, so there would always be a long line of people who had come to taste the original *oyakodon* for lunch.

I sometimes went to the restaurant with my colleagues, but to tell the truth, I did not care for *oyakodon* that much. Let me tell you why. When I was young, my grandmother was sick and had to stay in bed for several years. For some reason unknown to me, she would often insist on getting *oyakodon* delivered for her lunch from a small noodle restaurant nearby, even when her meal was prepared at home. But in order to make a delivery, the restaurant required that customers order at least two portions of the dish. As a result, one of us had to eat the other portion of *oyakodon* that was delivered. This experience turned me off *oyakodon* as I was made to eat it too often.

Consequently, I do not cook *oyakodon* very often, with the paradoxical result that *oyakodon* has become one of my children's favourite dishes. I serve it only on days when I am very busy or when I'm short of time. Thus, the relative rarity of *oyakodon* on my dining table has secured it its position as a cherished dish for my children.

By the way, do you know the name of the dish if sliced pork or beef is used in place of chicken? It is called *tanindon* (stranger bowl), as pork and beef have no relation to eggs. Besides chicken and egg *oyakodon,* there also is a seafood *oyakodon* that is topped with salmon and *ikura* (salmon roe).

Oyakodon Serves 4

1 onion

400 g (14 oz) chicken

a handful of *mitsuba* leaves

240 ml (1 cup) dashi stock (page 127)

4 Tbsp Japanese soy sauce

4 Tbsp mirin

6 eggs

4 *donburi* bowls, about two-thirds filled with cooked Japanese rice (page 126)

1. Peel the onion and slice thinly. Cut the chicken into bite-size pieces. Cut the *mitsuba* into 4-cm (1¹/₂-inch) lengths.

2. Pour the dashi into a large frying pan and add the soy sauce and mirin. Bring to a boil over medium heat. Add the onion and chicken. Cook, covered, for 4–5 minutes or until heated through.

3. While the chicken-and-onion mixture is cooking, break the eggs into a bowl and beat lightly. Pour the eggs into the pan over the chicken-and-onion mixture. Sprinkle the *mitsuba* on top of the chicken and eggs. Continue to cook, covered, for a further minute and remove from heat before eggs have fully set. Top each bowl of rice with a quarter of the cooked chicken-and-egg mixture.

A gourmet treat in a seaside town

During the winter, we use a *donabe*, an earthenware pot which we use for cooking over heat on the table, at least once a week. Of my *nabe* recipes, I am sure that the most popular among my family members is salmon *nabe* flavoured with miso and garlic.

This is a recipe which I learnt in Kamakura, a seaside resort just outside Tokyo that was the capital of Japan in ancient times. The company my husband works for has a small Japanese-style inn there where employees can stay at a very reasonable price while enjoying the historic town. When our children were younger, we stayed at the inn from time to time.

The young lady who used to manage the place would always welcome us with wonderful hospitality. Her husband, a professional cook, would serve us various kinds of wonderful gourmet dishes for dinner. At every meal, beautiful appetizers and fresh sashimi would be neatly arranged on the table, and tasty dishes were carefully served one by one at the perfect temperature.

Once, we were served salmon, seafood, chicken, vegetables and mushrooms in a large *donabe* placed on a portable gas burner. That was the first time we tasted the miso-and-garlic salmon pot and we all loved it. Whenever we visited the inn, I would always look forward to dinnertime.

When we visited Kamakura last year for the first time after a long while, the inn had been nicely remodelled, but we were disappointed to find that the couple had left and a Western-style menu was served in place of the gourmet Japanese-style dishes we loved.

Now at home, whenever we prepare this salmon *nabe*, we often think about the young lady with her heartwarming smile and the wonderful food we enjoyed so much.

QUICK STOCK If konbu is not available, the stock can be made with 800 ml (3$^1/_3$ cups) of water and 2 tsp of instant dashi, or prepare according to the manufacturer's directions.

SUBSTITUTE FOR CHRYSANTHEMUM GREENS If you are unable to get hold of chrysanthemum greens, spinach makes a good substitute.

Salmon Nabe with Miso and Garlic   Serves 6

800 ml (3¹/₃ cups) water

10 g (¹/₃ oz) died konbu, about
5 x 15 cm (2 x 6 inch)

3 potatoes

4 salmon fillets

6 boiled scallops

300 g (10¹/₂ oz) chicken thigh

300 g (10¹/₂ oz) block soft tofu,
drained (see Note on page 14)

¹/₄ head Chinese cabbage

100 g (3¹/₂ oz) edible
chrysanthemum greens

2 leeks

100 g (3¹/₂ oz) enoki or *shimeji*
mushrooms

5–6 Tbsp miso

2 cloves garlic, peeled and grated

butter, to serve

shichimi togarashi

udon noodles, optional

1. Pour the 800ml (3¹/₃ cups) of water into a *donabe*. Wipe the konbu with a damp cloth and let soak in the *donabe*.

2. In another pot, boil the potatoes until tender, then peel and slice into 1-cm (¹/₂-inch) thick rounds. Cut each salmon fillet into 3 pieces. Cut the scallops into halves. Cut the chicken and the tofu into bite-size pieces. Wash the Chinese cabbage, cut into half lengthwise, then into 5-cm (2-inch) pieces. Discard the hard ends of the chrysanthemum greens and cut into 5-cm (2-inch) pieces. Slice the white part of the leeks diagonally into 5-cm (2-inch) lengths. Discard the hard part of the mushroom stalks. Arrange all the ingredients on a large plate.

3. Place a portable gas burner on the table and heat up the *donabe* containing the water and konbu over medium-high heat. Just before the stock starts boiling, remove and discard the konbu. Add the miso and mix well. Add the garlic. Add portions of the salmon and handfuls of the other ingredients and cook until heated through, covering with a lid until the pot starts to boil. Remove each batch of ingredients from the *donabe* as they cook and serve immediately with a piece of butter and *shichimi togarashi*. Keep replacing the ingredients in the *donabe* until everyone has eaten their fill, occasionally skimming any foam or fat from the pot. If the ingredients are getting overcooked, turn the heat to low. After the solid ingredients are almost gone, you can cook udon noodles in the remaining soup for a flavourful second course.

Affordable Feasts and Fuel for Footballers

Soup to fuel soccer players

During the New Year's holiday, my younger children worked on their *kakizome*, or New Year's writing, a popular Japanese tradition. *Kakizome* literally means the start of writing, as the word is a combination of *kaku* (to write) and *someru* (to start). Similarly, the weaning ceremony for babies is called *okuizome*, combining the word *someru* with the honorific prefix *o* and *kui* (eating).

Meanwhile, a closing ceremony is often called *osame*, as the verb *osameru* means to close or complete. Thus, the final working day of the year is called *shigoto* (work) *osame*. At the end of last year, my younger sons' soccer club held a *keriosame* event, marking the year's final practice. *Keriosame* is a combination of the words *keru* (to kick) and *osameru*.

Well, that final kick was nothing like a formal event, but more than 150 children in the club enjoyed games and were served special snacks. Many parents also participated in the event and played soccer with the children. The event started in the morning and lasted until the evening.

My second son, who is in the sixth grade at elementary school, is one of the oldest members of the team. He returned home late after the *keriosame* event as he had helped to organize it. As soon as he came through the door, he happily reported that all the sixth-graders were served *tonjiru* (miso soup with pork and vegetables) as their special reward. In his excitement, he could not stop repeating, "I have never had such tasty *tonjiru*. Although your *tonjiru* is quite tasty, Mom, that *tonjiru* served today was the best I've had."

I don't blame him for saying that. I'm sure that hot *tonjiru* served outdoors in freezing weather must be one of the best winter foods there is. I usually serve *tonjiru* in a comfortably heated room, and I always make a large pot so that the children can eat as much as they want. In contrast, the portion of *tonjiru* served after the *keriosame* was probably limited, and the children, who had been out in the cold and exhausted after a full day of activity, naturally felt that the soup was precious, which must have given extra spice to the *tonjiru* that day.

I usually use *satoimo* (taro) in *tonjiru*, but my son's favourite is made with potatoes. Once everyone has had their fill of the soup, I like to add some cooked rice to the leftovers to serve in the form of *zosui* (Japanese risotto). I sometimes also use the leftover soup as a base for miso-flavoured udon with pork and vegetables. These dishes are very good for a warm lunch the following day.

Tonjiru   Serves 8–10

170 g (6 oz) block *konnyaku*

$^1/_2$ burdock root

1 Tbsp vinegar

300 g (10$^1/_2$ oz) thinly sliced
 pork rib meat

5-cm (2-inch) length daikon radish

1 carrot

2 potatoes

140 g (5 oz) *atsuage* deep-fried tofu

1 leek

1 Tbsp vegetable oil

2 litres (8 cups) water

2 tsp instant dashi powder

5–6 Tbsp miso of your choice

1. Cut the *konnyaku* lengthwise into 4 strips. Cut each strip into 3-mm (1$^1/_5$-inch) thick pieces. Cook in boiling water for 2–3 minutes and drain. Scrape the burdock root with the back of a knife to remove the brown surface, then wash with water. Cut into 1-cm ($^1/_2$-inch) pieces. Leave in a bowl of water with the vinegar until ready to use.

2. Cut the pork into 2-cm ($^3/_4$-inch) wide pieces. Peel and cut the daikon and carrot into 5-mm ($^1/_4$-inch) thick fan-shaped pieces. Peel the potatoes and cut into 1-cm ($^1/_2$-inch) thick fan-shaped pieces. Cut the *atsuage* into half lengthwise and cut into 5-mm ($^1/_4$-inch) thick slices. Cut the leek into 1-cm ($^1/_2$-inch) pieces.

3. In a large pot, heat the vegetable oil over medium heat. Add the drained burdock and carrot and sauté. Add the pork and stir-fry until the colour changes. Add the water, daikon, potatoes and *konnyaku* and bring to a boil. Add the dashi powder and simmer for 15–20 minutes until the potatoes and carrots are tender, constantly skimming foam from the surface of the stock. Add the *atsuage* and leek. Stir in the miso and cook for 2–3 minutes. Serve hot.

Oshiruko sweet bean soup to make someone happy

When my daughter was in kindergarten, she came home one winter's day and announced, "My teacher said we will have an *oshirikko taikai* tomorrow." She was quite excited about the special event, but did not know what it was about.

I was at a complete loss as the term *oshirikko taikai* literally means kids' bottom event. I wondered if it would involve hip wrestling (*shiri zumo*) and thought she might need to wear warm underwear to take part in the event which would probably be held outdoors.

I asked her, "Did your teacher tell you to bring anything for the *oshirikko taikai*?" She immediately replied, "A wooden soup bowl and a pair of chopsticks!" This solved the riddle. "Well," I said, "I think you mean an *oshiruko taikai*, not an *oshirikko taikai*, is that right?" She shrugged, "Something like that."

The *oshiruko taikai* was an annual event where the kindergarten teachers would prepare a huge pot of *oshiruko*—sweet azuki bean soup with mochi rice cakes or *shiratama dango* dumplings—for the children.

My daughter came home the next day and happily told me that the *oshiruko* was so tasty she had two bowls of it. In winter, warm, sweet *oshiruko* with mochi makes everybody happy, and in Japan, *oshiruko* is often served after sports events and other outdoor activities.

Now, 10 years on, my daughter is a middle school student. On a very cold day in January this year, there was a television news report about a middle school entrance exam held at Makuhari Messe, a large convention hall in Chiba, just outside Tokyo. Thousands of children took the exam including some of my children's friends.

Excited by the news, I started cooking *oshiruko*. The small red azuki beans simmering in the pot brought to mind the children, with their faces flushed, filling in their answer sheets for the very competitive exam. I prayed for them while making *oshiruko* and took a pot of it to the home of one of the children I knew afterward. (I was so glad to know he passed the exam!)

Oshiruko is a winter food typically prepared when you cannot find anything else to do for someone who is striving for something, and you want to cheer the person on. I am sure I will have many more chances to prepare *oshiruko* while my children are growing up.

Oshiruko   Serves 8–10

300 g (10½ oz) dried azuki beans
  and enough water to cover beans

2 litres (8 cups) water

200 g (7 oz) sugar

a pinch of salt

8–10 pieces mochi rice cake or
  16–20 pieces boiled *shiratama
  dango* dumplings (page 77)

1. Wash the azuki beans and drain. Put the beans in a
   pot and add enough water to cover. Bring to a boil and
   simmer for 5–10 minutes and drain. Return the beans
   to the pot, add the 2 litres (8 cups) of water and bring
   to a boil. Lower the heat and simmer for 60–80 minutes
   until the beans are completely tender. While simmering,
   occasionally skim off the foam and add more water as
   the liquid reduces. Add the sugar and salt and gently stir
   to dissolve. Simmer for another 10 minutes and remove
   from heat.

2. If using mochi rice cakes, cut them into halves and grill
   until puffy and brown. Serve the hot azuki bean soup
   in individual wooden bowls with grilled mochi or boiled
   shiratama dango.

103

An affordable feast for even the most ravenous of children

Shabu-shabu is a delicious one-pot dish that my whole family enjoys. However, there is a problem: quality beef, thinly sliced for shabu-shabu, is very expensive. As such, we have shabu-shabu only on special occasions.

My youngest son loves the dish so much that he insisted a few years ago that he would use his *otoshidama* (New Year's gift money) to buy a special copper shabu-shabu pot for our shabu-shabu meals. Unfortunately, the pot was too expensive and we still use a regular *donabe* (an earthenware pot) whenever we have shabu-shabu.

When I was a child, my grandmother would invite all her children and their families to her house during the New Year's holiday and she would prepare a large amount of vegetables, tofu and two different plates of special sliced beef for both sukiyaki and shabu-shabu. She would place two portable gas burners on a large table—one to be used for sukiyaki and the other for shabu-shabu. Those who preferred sukiyaki would choose a seat close to the sukiyaki pot, and those who preferred shabu-shabu would choose one close to the shabu-shabu pot. I loved to sit between the two pots and enjoy both dishes. It was great fun for us kids as we could eat endlessly. But the tradition ended with my grandmother's death 14 years ago.

At the end of last year, for the first time in a long while, my mother invited the family, including my cousins, their spouses and children over for a meal. There were 24 of us altogether. On the menu were sukiyaki and shabu-shabu of course! News of the special party made us so happy and the children were naturally very excited.

Shabu-shabu does not have to be made with beef. Pork shabu-shabu with lettuce is a great recipe I learnt from my mother. It is easy to prepare and as pork is cheaper than beef, you can buy enough for ravenous children without worrying about the cost. You will be surprised, too, by the quantity of lettuce that will be consumed. I also serve it with a peanut butter sauce— which I created when we were out of store-bought sesame sauce—and it was a big hit with the children.

HOME-MADE PEANUT BUTTER SAUCE Store-bought sesame sauce or ponzu sauce can be substituted with this special home-made peanut butter sauce.

Pork Shabu-shabu with Lettuce   Serves 4

Shabu-shabu

10 g (1/3 oz) died konbu, about
   5 x 15 cm (2 x 6 inch)

1 litre (4 cups) water

1 head lettuce

300 g (10 1/2 oz) block soft tofu,
   drained (see Note on page 14)

1 leek

140 g (5 oz) enoki mushrooms

800 g (1 3/4 lb) thinly sliced pork

Peanut Butter Sauce

130 g (4 1/2 oz) peanut butter

120 ml (1/2 cup) hot dashi stock
   (page 127)

120 ml (1/2 cup) ponzu sauce

1. Wipe the konbu with damp cloth. Pour the 1 litre (4 cups) of water into a casserole dish, shabu-shabu pot or *donabe* and add the konbu. Let soak. Cut off and discard the hard parts of the lettuce and break the leaves into 3–4 pieces, then wash and drain. Cut the tofu in half lengthwise, then cut crosswise into 1-cm (1/2-inch) thick chunks. Discard the green part of the leek. Slice the white part diagonally into very thin slices. Cut off the hard bottom parts of the mushrooms. Place the pot on a portable gas burner and bring to a boil. Just before it starts boiling, remove and discard the konbu.

2. To make the peanut butter sauce, put the peanut butter into a bowl and add the hot dashi stock. Stir well with a fork until smooth. Add the ponzu and mix well. Serve in individual dipping bowls.

3. Cook the vegetables, tofu and pork slices at the table. Cook the lettuce leaves for about 10 seconds (making sure not to overcook them) and the pork for about 15 seconds or until the colour of the meat changes completely. Dip in the sauce and enjoy.

Football victory built on grandmother's recipe

In January, my eldest son, who is 17 years old, participated in an American football game. It was the Stick Bowl, a high school all-star game. The word Stick is an acronym formed from the names of five prefectures—Saitama, Tokyo, Ibaraki, Chiba and Kanagawa—and my son had dreamed of becoming a member of the Tokyo all-star team ever since he started playing American football.

The selection was held in November and my son was elated when he heard that he had been named a member of the Tokyo team. My parents were overjoyed when he phoned them with the news and they took him to a *yakiniku* grilled meat restaurant for a dinner treat.

During the winter vacation, the chosen players from the different high schools got together to train for the event. Despite being exhausted from the practices, my son was fulfilled and satisfied.

One evening, four days before the Stick Bowl, I received a phone call from my mother. She had made something special for my son and wanted me to go pick it up. At her house, she handed me a wrapped container that was warm to the touch and there was a wonderful aroma coming from it. When I got home and opened the container, I found four huge meat patties inside, each coated with a golden sauce.

That evening, before my eldest son came home, my other children and I had dinner sharing three of the huge meat patties, setting one aside for him.

When I called and thanked my mother for the delicious meat patties, she was a little upset that we had eaten them and explained that all four patties were meant for my eldest son. She had created a special recipe considering his needs as an athlete and wanted him to eat one patty every day after practice until the big game. She had read that chicken breast meat contains elements that are very effective in helping athletes recover from fatigue, so she combined minced chicken, tofu, carrot, diced *nagaimo* (yam), sesame seeds and many other ingredients to make these special meat patties that were low in fat and high in protein.

Well, thanks in part to my mother's thoughtfulness, my son was able to help his team win the game. The chicken and *nagaimo* patties that were added to our family's trove of recipes will remind us of her warm-hearted support for her grandson. The sauce, made of balsamic vinegar, soy sauce and mirin is my creation, and I am sure that it would also go well with sautéed fish or meat.

SUBSTITUTE FOR NAGAIMO (YAM) If you can't get hold of *nagaimo*, omit it and double the quantity of onion.

Chicken and Nagaimo Patties   Makes 4 large or 8 medium patties

¹/₄ carrot

1 knob fresh ginger

¹/₂ onion

90 g (3 oz) block soft tofu

450 g (1 lb) minced chicken breast

1 egg

1 Tbsp toasted white sesame seeds

¹/₂ tsp salt

1 tsp oyster sauce

2 Tbsp cornflour (cornstarch)
  or *katakuriko*

100 g (3¹/₂ oz) *nagaimo* (yam)

1 Tbsp vegetable oil

2 Tbsp Japanese soy sauce

2 Tbsp balsamic vinegar

2 Tbsp mirin

1. Peel and grate the carrot and ginger. Peel and mince the onion. In a bowl, combine the grated carrot, ginger, tofu, onion and minced chicken. Mix well. Add the egg, sesame seeds, salt, oyster sauce and cornflour or *katakuriko* and mix well with your hands. Peel the *nagaimo* and dice finely. Combine the *nagaimo* and the chicken mixture and mix well. Form into 4 large or 8 medium patties. At this point, the chicken mixture is soft and may be a little difficult to handle, but the patties will become firmer when cooked through.

2. Heat the vegetable oil in a large frying pan over medium-high heat. Cook the patties for 1 minute over medium-high heat. Turn the patties over and reduce the heat to low. Cook, covered, for 12–13 minutes or until heated through.

3. Transfer the patties to individual serving plates, leaving the juices in the pan. Place the pan over medium heat and add soy sauce, balsamic vinegar and mirin to the juices to make a sauce. Heat for 30 seconds or until the sauce is reduced by about half. Serve the patties with the sauce and a side dish of vegetables.

107

Sea bream, an auspicious fish for a festive dish

In Japan, the school year starts in April and ends in March, and thus March is filled with school graduation ceremonies. As I have four children, I always seem to have a school ceremony to attend at this time of the year.

This year, my second son is going to graduate from elementary school and he received his new school uniform for middle school a few weeks ago. Dressed in his *tsume-eri* (boy's school uniform with a stand-up collar), he looked all grown-up.

As my children attend the same school I did, I know most of the farewell songs that are sung at the graduation ceremonies. Whenever I hear these songs, I think of the many graduations I've sat through, including my own, and so many memories come flooding back.

My second son's graduation will be just as touching and I will definitely cry when I see him receiving his diploma. (I might need a box of tissues and a large towel to get through the ceremony.)

For graduation day, I am planning to cook him a sea bream—called *tai* in Japanese. In Japan, a whole fish is traditionally served at celebratory banquets, such as wedding receptions. The dish is usually called *okashira-tsuki*. *O* means tail and *kashira* means head, and the phrase *okashira-tsuki* means the complete fish with tail and head, symbolizing the completeness of life. Sea bream is very much appreciated for the *okashira-tsuki* because the word *tai* has the same last syllable as the word *omedetai* (auspicious).

My recipe is different from the traditional method of simply grilling the sea bream with salt. Instead, I roast the sea bream with seasonal vegetables, and my children love the dish. I remember that I cooked the dish for my second son's first birthday dinner. Although he did not understand the significance behind the dish then, he was delighted as he looked at the large sea bream prepared especially for him. We still have a photograph of his beaming smile taken on that day.

Now, my children are grown and one sea bream is not enough to feed us all. However, I still feel happy whenever I prepare *okashira-tsuki* as it creates such an auspicious atmosphere at our family table on special days.

VEGETABLES In summer, I like to cook this dish with red, yellow and green bell peppers (capsicums) and courgettes (zucchinis). In winter, I like to use turnips.

VARIATION Steamed clams also go well with this dish. Instead of roasting the sea bream for 30 minutes, roast it for 20 minutes, then remove from the oven. Place 300 g (10½ oz) of cleaned clams around the fish and pour 100 ml (²/₅ cup) of white wine or sake over. Cover the casserole with aluminium foil, return to the oven and roast for another 10 minutes or until the shells open.

Roasted Sea Bream and Vegetables   Serves 4–6

2 cloves garlic

2 onions

1 large sea bream, about 1 kg (2$^{1}/_{4}$ lb)

1$^{1}/_{2}$ tsp salt

8–10 bay leaves

12 cherry tomatoes, trimmed

your choice of seasonal vegetables

2 Tbsp olive oil

$^{1}/_{2}$ lemon

1. Preheat the oven to 230°C (450°F). Peel and thinly slice the garlic cloves. Peel and cut the onions into 8 wedges each. Scale, wash and gut the sea bream. (Or ask the fish monger to do it for you.) Pat dry with a paper towel. Make 4 slits across the fish on both sides, cutting right down to the bones. Rub each side with $^{1}/_{2}$ tsp salt. Stuff the slits with the sliced garlic and the bay leaves.

2. Place the fish in a large casserole dish. Place the onion wedges, cherry tomatoes and other seasonal vegetables around the fish. Sprinkle the remaining $^{1}/_{2}$ tsp salt over the vegetables. Drizzle the olive oil over the fish and vegetables. Roast for 30 minutes in the preheated oven.

3. Remove the roasted fish and vegetables from the oven and serve with lemon wedges and the liquid in the casserole dish, which makes a very tasty sauce.

Takenoko sprout in spring, on mountainsides and in stores

At this time of the year, whole fresh *takenoko* (bamboo shoots) are on display at the grocery stores. Although they are heavy, expensive and time-consuming to prepare, I cannot ignore them as to me, they are the vegetables of spring. The other day, when I visited a supermarket, there were *takenoko* on display by the entrance and they were calling out to me as I walked by holding an empty shopping basket. Beside the pile of *takenoko*, there were packs of *nuka* (rice bran), for boiling with *takenoko* to remove its bitterness, and tiny young sprigs of *sansho* leaves, which are good to serve on top of *takenoko gohan* (rice cooked with bamboo shoots). I could not resist "team *takenoko*" and ended up buying a small *takenoko* from the pile. I decided to cook *takenoko gohan* that day as *takenoko* has to be cooked as soon as possible. If kept too long, it becomes hard and bitter.

Takenoko is delicate in its aroma and texture and it can be easily overwhelmed by a main dish with a strong flavour, thus I made the *takenoko gohan* part of a dinner menu that included lightly flavoured dishes such as simple grilled fish, spinach with sesame sauce and a clear soup.

When I was a child, my grandfather's friend used to invite us to dig for *takenoko* on the mountainside behind his house. We would use large shovels, being careful not to damage the *takenoko,* which was a tricky task. After the harvest, my mother would cook *takenoko* dishes for days on end.

Of course, the *takenoko* I bought at the supermarket the other day was too small to enjoy in more than one recipe. But yesterday, my neighbour brought us a freshly dug *takenoko* that was too large to fit even in my largest pot. My family and I will enjoy various *takenoko* dishes tonight, such as simmered *takenoko* and clear soup with wakame and *takenoko*.

VARIATION Add 140 g (5 oz) of diced chicken.

FRESH TAKENOKO To boil fresh *takenoko*, peel off 2–3 layers of the outer rind and make a diagonal cut to trim off about 4 cm (1 1/2 inch) of the tip. Cut off 1 cm (1/2 inch) of the bottom part and score the husk vertically with a knife, being careful not to cut the main body. Put the *takenoko* in a large pot and add water to cover. Add a handful of rice bran and a few pieces of dried red chilli to remove the bitterness. Bring to a boil and turn the heat to low. Simmer for 1 hour, adding water as needed. Remove from heat and let it cool in a pot with simmering water. When completely cool, wash the *takenoko* under running water and peel away the extra skin to reveal a buttery cream coloured layer.

READY-COOKED TAKENOKO If you're using canned or vacuum-packed boiled *takenoko*, rinse well, then cut into small pieces before cooking with the rice.

Takenoko Gohan   Serves 4

480 g (17 oz) uncooked Japanese
  rice

600 ml (2¹/₂ cups) dashi stock
  (page 127)

2¹/₂ Tbsp Japanese soy sauce

2¹/₂ Tbsp mirin

3 Tbsp sake

¹/₂ tsp salt

140 g (5 oz) boiled *takenoko*

1 slice *abura-age* (deep-fried tofu)

young *sansho* leaves, for garnish

1. Wash and drain the rice and place in a rice cooker or
   pot with the dashi stock, soy sauce, mirin, sake and salt.
   Gently stir and let sit for 30 minutes.

2. Cut the *takenoko* into small, thin pieces. Place the *abura-
   age* in a sieve and pour boiling water over to scald it.
   Drain, then cut into half lengthwise and into thin strips.

3. Place the *takenoko* and *abura-age* on top of the rice
   and smooth the surface. Cook the rice following the
   instructions on page 126. When cooked, gently fold the
   rice and ingredients with a wooden paddle to mix. Do this
   with gentle cutting motions to avoid mashing the rice.
   Serve in individual rice bowls and top with *sansho* leaves.

A simple recipe to fill a lunch box

I pack lunch in bento boxes for my older children every morning. My daughter, who goes to middle school, takes a regular-size bento and it is easy for me to fill it. However, I struggle to fill my 17-year-old son's bento as it is huge. He has an incredible appetite and the size of his bento box has been getting bigger and bigger. I often feel helpless trying to find food to fill up the extra space in his bento box.

My son says he gets hungry as soon as he arrives at school and he has to eat half of his packed lunch before lunchtime. This is called *hayaben* among schoolkids. The word is made up of two other words *hayai* (early) and bento, and it literally means eating bento before lunchtime, which is usually prohibited in schools. As my son snacks on his bento every morning, the portion left for his actual lunch is only about half, leaving him hungry again in the afternoon.

Last week, my son came home saying that he was starving as usual, and I was just getting ready to grill miso and yoghurt chicken for dinner. This is a dish I often prepare using chicken breast. I cut up and marinate the meat in a mixture of white miso and plain yoghurt in a plastic bag and leave it for a day or two before grilling it in the oven. I love how the combination of yoghurt and miso make the chicken breast so tender and savoury.

That day, as I had just bought some baguettes from a bakery, I decided to make my hungry son a chicken baguette sandwich with cheese, tomato, lettuce and avocado for his after-school snack.

He enjoyed it so much that he suggested I make a baguette sandwich for his bento the next day. The next morning, I made a sandwich with the same ingredients using a whole baguette and cut it into three pieces. He was finally content and said he would have one for *hayaben* and the other two as his regular lunch. For me, the large sandwich was a great idea I had never thought of before. Now, both of us are happy with this solution.

This miso and yoghurt chicken can be served as a main dish together with salad or other accompaniments. You can also combine it with your choice of other ingredients in a sandwich.

Miso and Yoghurt Grilled Chicken   Serves 4

4 Tbsp white miso

4 Tbsp plain yoghurt

2 chicken breasts, about 600 g
   (1¹/₃ lb)

¹/₄ tsp salt

ground white pepper

1. Put the miso and yoghurt in a thick plastic bag and massage the bag with your fingers to blend the miso and yoghurt well.

2. Cut the chicken into 1.5-cm (¹/₂-inch) thick slices and sprinkle with salt and pepper. Put the chicken slices into the plastic bag with the miso and yoghurt and massage the bag again with your fingers to coat the chicken slices completely with the mixture. Keep the plastic bag in the refrigerator overnight or for up to 2 days.

3. Preheat the oven to 200°C (400°F). Arrange the chicken in a single layer on a baking tray lined with parchment paper. Bake for 25–30 minutes or until the surface turns light golden and the chicken is heated through. The miso-coated surface of the chicken burns easily, so check the oven constantly and cover the chicken with aluminium foil if necessary. Remove to a serving plate and serve with a salad or other accompaniments.

Massive natsumikan oranges go over like a bomb

We have a *natsumikan* orange tree in our garden. My great grandmother raised it from a tiny seed from a *natsumikan* she had particularly enjoyed. As the tree grew larger, it bore more oranges, although the fruit became smaller in size as the years went by.

Last year, for the first time in a long while, we asked a gardener to prune the tree. After pruning, all the branches were exposed to sunlight and the new crop of fruit were much larger. A few weeks ago, my son cut the oranges from the tree using long pruning shears. I had a fright because the fruit fell to the ground like bombs, one after another.

In anticipation of our harvest, some of my neighbours had asked if they could have some of the fruit to make orange marmalade. Thus, I put some of the large oranges into paper bags and went out to deliver them. One of my neighbours was not home, and as it was getting late, I hung a bag of the oranges on her front door, so she would find it when she returned home.

The next morning, I heard voices coming from that neighbour's yard.

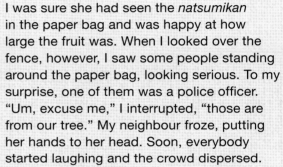

I was sure she had seen the *natsumikan* in the paper bag and was happy at how large the fruit was. When I looked over the fence, however, I saw some people standing around the paper bag, looking serious. To my surprise, one of them was a police officer. "Um, excuse me," I interrupted, "those are from our tree." My neighbour froze, putting her hands to her head. Soon, everybody started laughing and the crowd dispersed.

My neighbour had found the paper bag hanging on her front door. As there was no note attached, she phoned some friends to find out if they had put it there. None of them did and she called the police.

I apologized for causing so much trouble, reminding her that these were the oranges I had promised her. She laughed, and with tears in her eyes said, "I never thought it was from you—these oranges looked so much bigger than your normal *natsumikan!*"

With the alarmingly bomb-like *natsumikan*, I made a cool dessert for my children using the rind for cups. The sweet coconut milk and sour *natsumikan* make a good combination. The colour of the two layers of jelly looks cool when served in glasses too.

SUBSTITUTE FOR NATSUMIKAN JUICE If *natsumikan* is not available, use orange juice or other fruit juices.

Natsumikan and Coconut Jelly   Makes 6 glasses or 4 *natsumikan* cups

15 g (¹/₂ oz) gelatin powder
100 ml (²/₅ cup) water
4 *natsumikan* or large oranges
300 ml (1¹/₄ cups) milk
100 ml (²/₅ cup) heavy cream
50 g (1³/₄ oz) coconut milk powder
110 g (4 oz) + 75 g (2¹/₂ oz) sugar

1. In a cup, soak the gelatin in the water. Segment the *natsumikan*, separating the flesh carefully from the rind, so that the rind can be used as serving cups. Squeeze the *natsumikan* or oranges and strain to extract 240 ml (1 cup) juice.

2. In a saucepan, combine the milk, heavy cream, coconut milk powder and 110 g (4 oz) sugar. Remove the pan from the heat before the mixture starts boiling and add two-thirds of the gelatin-and-water mixture. Stir well. Let the liquid cool to lukewarm. Using a ladle, spoon the coconut mixture into 6 glasses or 4 *natsumikan* cups (placed into bowls to keep them upright) until they are about two-thirds full. Leave to set in the refrigerator.

3. In a saucepan, heat the *natsumikan* or orange juice with 75 g (2¹/₂ oz) sugar until it comes to a boil. Turn off the heat. Add the remaining gelatin-and-water mixture. Stir well. Let cool.

4. When the coconut mixture has set, gently pour the *natsumikan* or orange juice mixture equally over the coconut mixture. Refrigerate until set. Serve chilled.

An ugly vegetable that makes a beautiful ratatouille

During the summer vacation, my youngest son grew some *goya*—known also as bitter gourd or bitter melon—in a flowerpot at home. When I was in elementary school, I used to grow *hechima* (loofah). Today, *goya* has taken the place of *hechima* and all four of my children have grown it at school. They water the plant every day and observe how it grows. They also sketch the plant from time to time and write down what they notice about it. It is a standard practice in science class and there is a quiz about the growth process of the *goya* plant during the semester.

When I was younger, *goya* was a specialty of Okinawa, the chain of semi-tropical islands at Japan's southernmost point, and it was hardly ever found at supermarkets in my neighbourhood. The first time I saw it, the awful appearance of the plant was shocking. Its green skin, covered with wart-like bumps was hardly appetizing, and when I did try it, it was incredibly bitter. However, I soon cultivated a taste for it, and now I find the *goya's* bitterness quite tasty.

The other day, when I visited a friend's apartment, I saw that her window was covered with greenery. It was a lovely natural shade of green made up of *goya* plants. She had planted them in containers placed on her balcony and let the vines climb up a large net which she had hung on the outer wall. I thought it was clever how she achieved two aims at once. The foliage provided a natural shade from the strong sunshine in the summer, doing away with the need for air conditioning. It also provided food for the table. She gave me one of the vegetables and I was able to enjoy it too.

The dish I most often prepare using this vegetable is *goya chanpuru*, a traditional Okinawan stir-fry of thinly sliced *goya*, pork, tofu and eggs. Recently, I tried adding *goya* and bacon to a ratatouille. As *goya* goes well with pork, it tasted as good as I thought it would. If you like the flavour of *goya*, you can have fun creating your own dish with this unique vegetable.

STORING AND SERVING RATATOUILLE Ratatouille will keep for up to 3 days in the refrigerator. Try serving it chilled with egg dishes such as omelettes or poached eggs for breakfast. For dinner I often serve it simply with grilled meat or fish.

Ratatouille with Goya and Bacon   Serves 8–10

1 medium *goya* (bitter gourd
  or bitter melon)

5 medium tomatoes

5 slices bacon

1 clove garlic

2 onions

2 courgettes (zucchinis)

6 medium eggplants (aubergines)

6 bell peppers (capsicums), a mix
  of red, yellow and green

3 Tbsp olive oil

1 bouillon cube

3 bay leaves

2 tsp salt

ground black pepper

1. Cut off both ends of the *goya,* then cut in half lengthwise. Scoop out and discard the seeds and spongy parts, which are very bitter. Cut into 1-cm ($^1/_2$-inch) thick slices and soak in a bowl of salted water. Peel the tomatoes and cut into wedges. Cut the bacon into 2-cm ($^3/_4$-inch) strips. Peel and chop the garlic. Peel and cut the onion into 8 wedges. Cut the ends off the courgettes and the caps off the eggplants. Slice the courgettes and eggplants into 2-cm ($^3/_4$-inch) thick disks. Remove the stems and seeds from the bell peppers and cut into bite-size pieces.

2. Drain the *goya*. In a large frying pan, heat 1 Tbsp olive oil and add the garlic. Add the *goya* and bacon and cook for 2–3 minutes over medium heat. Add the onion and cook for 1–2 minutes. Put the *goya*, bacon and onion into a large pot. In the frying pan, heat another 1 Tbsp olive oil and cook the eggplant and courgette for 2–3 minutes. Transfer them to the pot. Repeat the process with the bell peppers and the remaining oil.

3. Add the bouillon cube, bay leaves and tomatoes to the pot. Add the salt and pepper. Bring to a boil. Cook, covered, for 10 minutes over medium heat. Remove the lid and cook for another 10 minutes, stirring occasionally. Allow to cool, then chill in the refrigerator before serving.

The indispensable mentsuyu sauce

In August, my family and I spent two weeks in Vancouver on vacation. When we travel, we rarely stay at hotels as I like to cook for my children myself. (The main reason is that they eat so much.) Thus, we stayed in an apartment with a kitchen while we were there.

Before I left Japan, I bought a large amount of Japanese food, including nori, *furikake* (dried toppings for cooked rice), *somen* and soba noodles, mochi rice cakes, bottles of ponzu sauce and *mentsuyu* noodle sauce and packs of *mugicha* barley tea.

The items I thought would be most useful were the dried noodles and the bottle of instant *mentsuyu*. Store-bought *mentsuyu*, made up of dashi, soy sauce and mirin, can be used with various Japanese-style dishes. It works not only as a dipping sauce for noodles or tempura, but also as a simmering sauce for *nikujaga* (braised potatoes and beef) and for many varieties of *donburi* dishes.

The night before we left, I weighed the suitcase containing the food items and realized that I had to remove 1 kg (2¼ lb) worth of items to avoid the airline's surplus weight charge. Without thinking, and not wanting to spoil the perfectly packed suitcase, I removed the bottle of *mentsuyu*, as it was the exact weight I needed to remove.

I came to rue the decision to leave the *mentsuyu* at home. In Vancouver, we didn't have time to find Asian stores where we might have been able to buy Japanese seasonings such as mirin or dashi powder to make my own *mentsuyu* sauce. But my parents came to the rescue when they flew in to join us for the second week of our trip, and brought me a bottle of *mentsuyu*.

As *mentsuyu* is made from basic Japanese seasoning ingredients, it can also be used as a base for preparing other Japanese dishes.

When we returned from Vancouver, the rice season had arrived and fresh, tasty rice was aplenty. At the request of my children, I cooked their favourite *agedashi dofu* (deep-fried tofu) and seasonal grilled *sanma*. Both dishes go well with rice, and everybody enjoyed the taste of autumn.

The sauce for *agedashi dofu* is made from the same ingredients as for *mentsuyu* —dashi, soy sauce and mirin. In place of this sauce, you can use 240 ml (1 cup) of store-bought *mentsuyu* diluted with water.

USING MENTSUYU *Mentsuyu* usually has to be diluted with water. Follow the manufacturer's directions if using store-bought *mentsuyu*.

VARIATION Instead of deep-frying the tofu, you can also sauté it. To do this, dust it with cornflour (cornstarch), then sauté it in vegetable oil for 7–8 minutes over medium heat, turning it over occasionally.

Agedashi Dofu Serves 4

160 ml (²/₃ cup) dashi stock
(page 127)

3 Tbsp Japanese soy sauce

3 Tbsp mirin

300 g (10¹/₂ oz) block soft tofu,
drained (see Note on page 14)

4 eggplants (aubergines)

8 *shishito* peppers

vegetable oil for deep-frying

4 Tbsp cornflour (cornstarch)
or *katakuriko*

100 g (3¹/₂ oz) grated daikon radish,
for garnish

1 tsp grated fresh ginger,
for garnish

1. To make the sauce, put the dashi stock, soy sauce,
and mirin in a saucepan and bring to a simmer.

2. Cut the tofu into 8 pieces. Place on a paper towel and
drain well. Remove the caps of the eggplants and cut the
eggplants lengthwise into halves. Make small slits in the
shishito peppers with a sharp knife. Pat the vegetables dry
with paper towels. In a wok or deep-frying pan, heat the
vegetable oil to 180°C (350°F) and deep-fry the eggplants
for 1 minute. Drain. Reheat the oil and deep-fry the *shishito*
for 30 seconds. Drain.

3. Dust the tofu cubes with cornflour, then deep-fry until
light golden, turning once. Drain. Arrange the deep-fried
tofu and vegetables in individual bowls. Pour the hot
sauce over the tofu and serve garnished with grated
daikon and ginger.

Lotus, at the root of a savoury dish, perfect for a bento box

Our summer vacation in Vancouver, Canada meant that our two younger boys missed two weeks of soccer practice and games at home in Japan, and they were unhappy about that. During our first week in Vancouver, my sons brought along soccer balls and cleats wherever we went. Even when we went to a botanical garden, they had soccer balls in their backpacks, "just in case." They exerted steady pressure on me to take them to parks.

In the second week, I sent them off to a local tennis and soccer camp. It turned out to be a great idea. They played tennis in the morning and soccer in the afternoon. (My sons can be likened to tuna fish which die if they stop swimming.) My daughter, who is in her school's tennis team, also kept herself busy with intensive tennis lessons. Thus, while my children were enjoying sports, I found some time to relax.

However, one thing annoyed me. I had to get up early every morning to make bento boxes for their lunch. Although they were happy with sandwiches on the first day, they started missing Japanese-style bento. I made rice balls, but the variety of non-rice items in the bento was limited as I did not know where to shop for the Japanese ingredients I am familiar with. Despite this, we had a great two weeks, but when I saw a sign for bento in the airport food court on our way home, I could not resist getting it for our final lunch in Canada. Everyone was so happy with the warm rice and soy sauce-flavoured dishes.

Now that school has started, I am back to packing bento boxes every day. Among the most popular bento dishes in my family is one made with *renkon* (lotus root). We call the dish *renkon no kinpira*, but as I also use beef and pine nuts, the dish looks more like stir-fried beef with *renkon*. I like this dish as it can be used to fill the extra space in a bento box as a side dish, and it can also become the main dish if you add some extra beef. It is especially good served with other dishes, such as *tamagoyaki* rolled omelette and boiled green vegetables. It also keeps well in the refrigerator. When I cook this dish, I find that thinly sliced, good quality beef brings out the flavour best.

VARIATION A teaspoon of oyster sauce, added with the soy sauce and mirin, adds an extra dash of flavour.

PREPARING RENKON *Renkon* (lotus root) can be found in Asian grocery stores, either fresh, parboiled or frozen. Always soak it in vinegared water before using, to prevent discolouration.

Renkon no Kinpira   Serves 4–6

400 g (14 oz) *renkon* (lotus root)

1 Tbsp vinegar

200 g (7 oz) thinly sliced beef loin

1 knob fresh ginger

1 dried red chilli

1 Tbsp sesame oil

2 Tbsp Japanese soy sauce

2 Tbsp mirin

2 Tbsp pine nuts

1. Peel the *renkon* and slice thinly. Cut into fan-shaped pieces. Place in a large bowl and cover well with plenty of water mixed first with 1 Tbsp vinegar. Cut the beef into small pieces. Peel and mince the ginger. Slice the dried chilli and discard the seeds, which are extremely hot. Slice the seeded dried chilli very thinly.

2. In a frying pan, heat the sesame oil and add the ginger. Add the beef and cook over medium heat until the colour changes. Drain the *renkon* and add to the pan. Add the dried chilli. Cook for 5 minutes, stirring constantly with a wooden spatula. Add soy sauce and mirin and cook until almost all the liquid has evaporated. Sprinkle with pine nuts. Dish out and serve.

Gather gingko nuts with care

Huge gingko trees grow around my daughter's middle school, littering the ground with gingko nuts. My daughter says they stink. However, when I attended her school festival earlier this month, I noticed that the neatly packed gingko nuts were quickly sold out as they were very popular among the visiting mothers.

When I was little, my grandmother took me to collect gingko nuts scattered on the grounds of a nearby temple. She had me use chopsticks to pick the gingko nuts as direct contact with the flesh of the nuts can trigger allergic reactions. She herself wore rubber gloves, then placed the nuts in plastic nets As a child, I was fascinated to see her dig a hole in her yard, where she left the gingko nuts buried for about 10 days. When she dug them out and rinsed the net in a bucket of water, the soft outer skin of the nuts came off easily as she rubbed them through the net with gloved hands. With the soft outer layer rubbed away, only the hard inner nuts remained in the net.

The other day, my aunt told me that while this was a good way of getting rid of the foul-smelling soft outer layer of the gingko nuts, one of her friends had forgotten to dig the nuts up after burying them and they sprouted! She suggested that an easier method is to submerge a plastic net full of fresh gingko nuts in water and leave it for a few days. The softened outer layer can then be removed the same way my grandmother did and the cleaned nuts left to dry in the sun. But the preparation process does not end there. The hard shells have to be cracked with a hammer before they are roasted. The shells are then removed and the nuts boiled before the thin brown skin is peeled away to reveal the beautiful green jewels!

My grandmother used to make me tasty *chawan mushi* (steamed egg custard) using gingko nuts. Although I always wanted more, she put just a few in each individual cup as it is thought that gingko nuts can be toxic if taken in large quantities.

Although they are time-consuming and potentially hazardous to prepare, the beautiful gingko nuts, like pieces of edible jade, are still well worth the effort. Instead of going through the laborious collection and preparation process, you can buy nuts in their shells or even canned boiled ones, which are a lot easier to prepare.

STEAMING To cook *chawan mushi* without a steamer, cover the prepared cups with aluminium foil. Fill a wide-mouth pot with water up to 2.5-cm (1-inch) high and bring to a boil. Turn off the heat and place the cups in the water. Cover the pot and let the *chawan mushi* steam for about 10 minutes.

HANDLING GINGKO NUTS When handling fresh gingko nuts, wear rubber gloves to avoid touching the soft outer layer of the nuts which can trigger allergic reactions.

Chawan Mushi   Serves 4

4 small prawns (shrimp)

salt, as needed

sake, as needed

100 g (3¹/₂ oz) chicken fillet

Japanese soy sauce, as needed

2 fresh shiitake mushrooms

400 ml (1²/₃ cups) dashi stock
  (page 127)

3 eggs

4 slices *kamaboko* fish cake

8 cooked gingko nuts (available in
  cans or jars)

mitsuba leaves and yuzu rind,
  for garnish

1. Shell and devein the prawns. Sprinkle with a little salt
   and sake. Cut the chicken into 8 pieces and sprinkle
   with drops of soy sauce. Discard the stems of the
   shiitake and cut the caps into quarters.

2. Combine the dashi stock with ¹/₂ tsp salt, 1 Tbsp sake
   and 1 tsp soy sauce in a saucepan. Heat the dashi until
   the salt dissolves. Remove from the heat and leave to
   cool to room temperature.

3. Break the eggs into a large bowl and gently stir. Add the
   dashi to the eggs and mix. Strain the mixture through a
   sieve to make it smooth.

4. Into each of 4 heatproof cups, place 1 prawn, 1 slice
   of fish cake, 2 gingko nuts, 2 pieces of shiitake and
   2 pieces of chicken. Pour the dashi and egg mixture
   over the solid ingredients.

5. Steam in a preheated steamer over low heat for
   10–12 minutes or until the egg mixture sets. Garnish
   with *mitsuba* leaves and yuzu rind before serving.

New Year's dish, a marriage of different flavours

It's hard to believe that New Year's Day is just next week. When I was a child, my mother was busy at this time of year preparing *osechi ryori*, the special dishes to be enjoyed on the first day of the year. Among her seasonal kitchen tasks, she never forgot to cook what she called *yakitori*. Her *yakitori* was not the typical grilled chicken skewers. She made it with chicken thighs soaked in a mixture of soy sauce, mirin and grated ginger, and she would grill the chicken on New Year's Eve. Although she sometimes burned the chicken, she was happy with her *yakitori* which was a key component of her special *zoni*—a soup with chunks of mochi rice cake and other ingredients for the traditional New Year's Day breakfast.

There must be hundreds of *zoni* recipes across Japan. Basically, *zoni* with miso-based soup is common in the Osaka region and *zoni* with soy sauce-based clear soup is popular in the Tokyo region. In Osaka, many people use round pieces of rice cake for *zoni*, while in Tokyo, square pieces of rice cake are popular for the dish. Some people use grilled rice cake and others boiled rice cake.

Other ingredients, including local specialties, also differ from family to family. Newly married couples sometimes fight over *zoni* recipes, but some of them end up creating a new recipe by combining both family recipes.

As my mother's *zoni* contains so many ingredients—including grilled chicken, egg crêpe, *naruto* fish cake, spinach, bamboo shoots, dried mushrooms, nori, *mitsuba* and yuzu—I am sure that it is a recipe that came out of the marriages of my ancestors.

VARIATION My mother's *zoni* also contained slices of boiled bamboo shoot, blanched spinach and dried shiitake mushrooms. Grilled chicken can be replaced with chicken cooked in the soup.

Zoni Soup with Grilled Chicken   Serves 4

2 Tbsp mirin

2 Tbsp + 2 tsp Japanese soy sauce

1 tsp grated fresh ginger

200 g (7 oz) chicken thighs

salt, as needed

1.2 litres (5 cups) dashi stock
(page 127)

1 egg

8 mochi rice cakes

4 slices *naruto* fish cake or pink
kamaboko fish cake, each 5-mm
(1/4-inch) thick

4 sprigs *mitsuba*, for garnish

4 small pieces nori seaweed,
for garnish

4 slices yuzu rind, for garnish

1. Mix the mirin, 2 Tbsp soy sauce and ginger and use to
marinate the chicken. Set aside for at least 30 minutes.
Drain the chicken and grill until heated through. Let it
cool before cutting into bite-size slices.

2. Add 2 tsp soy sauce and 1 1/2 tsp salt to the dashi stock.

3. To make the egg crêpe, break the egg into a bowl. Add a
pinch of salt and stir well. Place a frying pan over medium
heat. Wipe the pan with an oil-soaked pad. Reduce the
heat and pour the egg into the pan, tilting the pan so the
egg is evenly spread. When the surface is set, flip it over
and cook for a few seconds. Remove from the pan and
cut into 8 pieces, each about 2 x 5-cm (3/4 x 2-inch).

4. Grill the mochi rice cakes until puffy and browned. In
each bowl, place 2 pieces of grilled rice cake, chicken,
and egg crêpe and 1 slice of fish cake. Pour the stock
over these ingredients and top with *mitsuba*, nori and
yuzu rind. Serve hot.

Basic Recipes

Japanese Rice
Makes about 1.2 kg (2²/₃ lb) cooked rice

480 g (17 oz) Japanese short-grain rice
water for rinsing
720 ml (3 cups) cold water

The precise amount of water needed to cook Japanese rice can vary according to whether the rice is newly harvested or has been on the shelves for a while. A general guideline is to use about 20 per cent more water than rice.

Whether cooking in a rice cooker or on the stove, Japanese rice needs to be rinsed well before cooking. Place the rice in a bowl with enough rinsing water to cover. Wash the rice once quickly by hand and immediately drain the cloudy water. Cover the rice with water again and wash by rubbing and mixing gently with your hands, then drain. Repeat this process 3 or 4 times until the water becomes almost clear. Drain the rice well in a fine-mesh strainer.

Using a Rice Cooker
Put the rinsed rice and the 720 ml (3 cups) of water into the rice cooker. Before pressing the start button, allow the rice to soak: 30 minutes in the summer and 1 hour in the winter, as rice absorbs water more easily when the weather is warm. (If you have one of the latest rice cookers that automatically calculates soaking time, you can skip this step).

In Japan non-wash rice (*musenmai*) is becoming popular. If you are using this kind of rice, I recommend rinsing it at least once because the rice and water quantities given in this book are for rice that has absorbed water from the rinsing process.

Using a Pot
Use a deep, heavy pot with a tight-fitting lid. The initial level of rice and water should be no more than a third of the pot's height, as the rice will expand during cooking.

Put the rinsed rice and the 720 ml (3 cups) of water in the pot and allow the rice to soak: 30 minutes in the summer and 1 hour in the winter, as rice absorbs water more easily when the weather is warm.

Cover the pot with the tight-fitting lid and bring to a boil over medium-high heat. When steam starts to escape from the pot, or it starts to boil over, turn the heat to low, and continue to cook, covered, for 15 minutes. Turn the heat to high for just a few seconds, then turn the heat off. Let the pot sit covered for 15 minutes to steam. Do not remove the lid until the whole process is completed.

Dashi Stock
Makes about 2 litres (8 cups) stock

20 g ($^2/_3$ oz) dried konbu
2 litres (8 cups) water
40 g ($1^1/_3$ oz) dried bonito flakes

I often make a large pot of dashi stock and keep it in the refrigerator to use over 2–3 days. You can also freeze the dashi, but it should be used within 3 weeks or the delicate flavour will be lost. I know of friends who freeze the dashi in ice cube trays, so they can use small portions as needed. Instant dashi stock powder is also available from supermarkets and you can prepare it according to the instructions on the pack.

To make dashi stock from scratch, wipe the konbu with a damp cloth. Pour the water into a pot and add the konbu. Let soak for 30 minutes to 1 hour, then place the pot over medium heat. Just before the stock starts boiling, remove the konbu and discard. Add the bonito flakes and bring to a boil. Skim off any foam. Turn off the heat and wait for 5 minutes or until all the bonito flakes sink. Strain the stock through a fine mesh strainer. For a clear, tasty stock, do not squeeze the bonito flakes. This recipe can be halved to make 1 litre of stock.

Glossary

Aonori
This edible seaweed is available in both dried and powdered form. It is typically used as a garnish and sprinkled over Japanese dishes just before serving.

Azuki Beans
Also spelled adzuki, these red beans are widely used in Asian cooking. They are often boiled with sugar to make red bean paste. They are available both dried and canned.

Benishoga
A Japanese pickle made of thinly sliced strips of ginger, coloured bright red. It is used as a garnish for a variety of dishes. Do not confuse it with *gari*, the pale pink, thinly slivered pickled ginger that is served with sushi.

Bonito Flakes
Known as *katsuobushi* in Japanese, these thin shavings of dried bonito fish are a key ingredient in dashi stock. Bonito flakes are also used as a garnish for vegetable or tofu dishes.

Burdock Root

Called *gobo* in Japanese, this long, thin root is typically sold in lengths measuring 40–50 cm (15–20 inches). Scrub it well, then scrape off the skin with a knife before using. To store, wrap it with moistened paper towels and place in a sealed plastic bag in the refrigerator.

Chrysanthemum Greens

Edible chrysanthemum greens are called *shungiku* in Japan, *chop suey* greens in the West and *tung oh* in Chinese. They are a popular addition to stews. Add them towards the end of cooking time, as they can become bitter if cooked too long.

Daikon Radish

This long, white root vegetable is widely used in Japanese cuisine, and can be eaten raw or cooked. Select roots that are firm, crisp and glossy, and free of blemishes.

Daikon Sprouts

These delicate sprouts have a slightly peppery flavour. They are eaten raw as they do not take well to cooking. You can find them in Asian grocery stores.

Dashi Stock

Dashi stock is the basis of many Japanese dishes. A recipe is provided on page 127 for home-made dashi stock. If pressed for time, instant dashi powder mixed with water is a useful substitute.

Eggplant

As known as aubergines, Japanese eggplants are smaller and thinner than Western varieties and are on average about 15-cm (6-inches) long. Unlike the Western varieties, Japanese eggplant does not require salting before use.

Enoki Mushrooms

Sold in clusters, these mushrooms are white in colour and have long and thin stems with tiny caps. They have a mild flavour and a crunchy texture. Select clusters that are firm and dry. Cut off the spongy root base (about 2.5-cm / 1-inch) before using.

Eringi mushrooms

Eringi mushrooms have plump, milky white stems and light brown caps. They have a mild flavour and a meaty, chewy texture. When buying, choose *eringi* that are firm and white with an elastic texture.

Fish Cake

Naruto and *kamaboko* are varieties of Japanese fish cake made from steamed white fish purée. They are available from Asian grocery stores.

Harusame Noodles

These thin, translucent noodles are very similar in appearance to bean thread noodles. Japanese *harusame* noodles are typically made from potato starch.

Japanese Rice

Japanese rice is a medium grain, glutinous rice. It is usually sold in its polished, white form. A recipe is provided on page 126 to make shiny, fluffy rice, with grains that stick together when cooked, and which can be easily picked up using chopsticks.

Japanese Soy Sauce

Due to differences in the brewing process, Japanese soy sauce tastes quite distinct from Chinese or other soy sauces. If possible, try to use Japanese soy sauce for the recipes in this book for an authentic Japanese falvour.

Kabocha Pumpkin

Also known as Japanese pumpkin, *kabocha* pumpkins have dark green skin and sweet dense flesh. It is used in both sweet and savoury dishes.

Katakuriko

This is Japanese potato starch which is used as a thickening agent in cooking. It can be hard to find outside Japan, but cornflour (cornstarch) makes an acceptable substitute although it is not as strong as *katakuriko*, so you may need to increase the quantity to achieve the thickening effect desired.

Konbu

This dried seaweed or kelp is a key element in dashi stock. When buying, choose konbu that is almost black in colour, thick and has a fine white powder on the surface which gives the konbu its flavour. Do not wash knobu before using, but wipe it with a cloth to clean it.

Konnyaku

Konnyaku is a grey jelly-like substance made from a tuber known as devil's tongue. It has no flavour, but is enjoyed for its texture. It is usually sold in the form of a square cake, packed in water and can be found in the refrigerated section of Japanese supermarkets.

Mirin

A type of cooking wine similar to cooking sake, mirin is typically used to give a sweet flavour and aroma to dishes.

Miso

There are many varieties of this fermented soy bean paste, and red and white miso are the two most common types. The recipes in this book use white miso, which has a milder flavour than the red.

Mitsuba

Also known as Japanese parsley, this green herb has a subtle flavour and is often used as a garnish. To store, wrap it with moistened paper towels and place in a sealed plastic bag in the refrigerator.

Mochi Rice Cake

This heavy, glutinous rice cake is made from rice flour, and is commonly sold in prepackaged blocks. When grilling mochi, grill until they expand and a crispy skin is formed. Grilled mochi can be served on its own with a soy sauce dip, nori or other topping. It can also be used as a topping for traditional soups.

Myoga

Myoga are the edible flower buds of the myoga plant. The buds have a fresh, gingery taste, and are sometimes available in Asian grocery stores.

Nagaimo (Yam)

This tuber has a cylindrical shape, and is typically about 8-cm (3-inches) in diameter. Choose roots that are firm and heavy with a flawless skin. To store, wrap it with moistened paper towels and place in a sealed plastic bag in the refrigerator. Cut off the portion required and peel only what is needed, as peeled *nagaimo* will lose its colour and flavour.

Nori

This edible seaweed is used as wrapping for sushi rolls and as a garnish. Nori is usually sold dried into thin flat sheets. Nori should be stored in a cool place in an airtight container.

Panko Breadcrumbs

These Japanese-style breadcrumbs are large, light and crispy. They are usually used as a coating for deep-fried foods. Panko breadcrumbs are available from supermarkets and Asian grocery stores.

Ponzu

This thin, citrus-based sauce, is typically used in marinades, as a dipping sauce, and for dressings. It is available in bottled form from supermarkets and Asian grocery stores.

Rice Vinegar

This Japanese distilled vinegar is made from rice wine, and has a mild flavour. It is available in bottled form from supermarkets and Asian grocery stores.

Sake

A widely used ingredient in Japanese cuisine, sake helps to lessen unpleasant odours in meat and fish. It can also help other ingredients absorb flavours better. Cooking sake is available in Asian grocery stores. It can be substituted with regular sake.

Sesame Oil

Extracted from toasted white sesame seeds, this fragrant oil adds a wonderful aroma to dishes it is used in. Buy in small quantities as sesame oil can go off quickly.

Sesame Seeds

Both black and white sesame seeds are widely used in Japanese cuisine, but the recipes in this book call for toasted white sesame seeds. The seeds can be bought ready toasted, but you can also toast raw sesame seeds yourself. Place a dry frying pan over low heat and shake the pan until the seeds start to pop.

Shichimi Togarashi

This essential Japanese tabletop condiment is made up of a mixture of seven spices including dried chillies. It is often sprinkled on noodles and soups to add spice and flavour.

Shiitake Mushrooms

These mushrooms are readily available fresh or dried. Store fresh shiitake in the refrigerator, wrapped in newspaper. Do not use a plastic bag as this will retain moisture and make the mushrooms slimy.

Shimeji Mushrooms

These mushrooms have grey caps and short, fat stems. Trim off the spongy part of the stem, about 2.5-cm (1-inch) from the base, before using. Rinse lightly to avoid diminishing the flavour.

Shiokonbu
Shiokonbu are strips of konbu that have been boiled in soy sauce and other ingredients, then dried and salted. *Shiokonbu* is available from Asian grocery stores.

Shiratamako Flour
Shiratamako flour is also known as sweet rice flour and it is available from Asian grocery stores.

Shishito Peppers
These small, mild peppers have thin, green skin. They are usually available in Asian grocery stores.

Shiso Leaves (Green)
Also known as perilla, Japanese basil and *oba*, green shiso leaves are available throughout the year. They are used as garnish for sashimi among other dishes. Shredded green shiso is often used as a topping for *hiyayakko* (cold tofu) and the whole leaves are often used as an edible wrapping for other ingredients.

Somen
These thin, white wheat noodles are usually sold dried and served cold, in the summer in Japan.

Tonkatsu Sauce
Also known as Japanese Worcester sauce, this condiment is available in bottled form in Asian grocery stores.

Udon
These thick, white, wheat noodles are usually sold dried and can be served hot or cold. They are a common addition to winter hotpots in Japan.

Umekonbucha
Umekonbucha is tea, flavoured with pickled plum and konbu. It is available from Asian grocery stores.

Wasabi
Also known as Japanese horseradish, wasabi is sold fresh, powdered or in paste form in tubes. The latter is convenient to use and is widely available.

Yuzu
The flesh of this small, round yellow-coloured citrus fruit is very sharp-tasting, and is not eaten, but its aromatic rind is used as a garnish and flavouring. Its juice can also be used in salad dressings and dipping sauces.

Recipe Index

Acknowledgements

Special thanks go to all who helped create this book:

To the team at Marshall Cavendish International (Asia), especially Lydia Leong, managing editor, for her efficient and reliable editing and attention to detail, and to Benson Tan, designer, for the lovely and cheerful layout.

To Noriko Yamaguchi, for her wonderful photographs and endless energy during the photography sessions.

To the staff at *The Japan News* (formerly *The Daily Yomiuri*), for giving me the opportunity to write my column these seven years.

To Deborah Iwabuchi and Cathy Lane, for opening the first door and encouraging me to step forward.

To Andrew White, and Ian and Lié Haffety for kindly putting me in touch with Marshall Cavendish International (Asia).

To Michael Staley of Staley Agency, for providing professional advice.

To Kazuhiko Ishikawa, Masato and Akane Tokunaga for offering unique pieces of pottery for the photographs.

To all my friends who appeared in the articles with their great recipes, helped me in the kitchen during the photography sessions.

To my parents, for always being so generous and supportive.

To my husband Akitomo, for his constant encouragement and technical assistance.

To my children, Shu, Hinako, Yu and Ken for always being hungry and providing me with so many stories over the years.